First World War
and Army of Occupation
War Diary
France, Belgium and Germany

19 DIVISION
Headquarters, Branches and Services
Royal Army Veterinary Corps
Assistant Director Veterinary Services
16 July 1915 - 30 November 1918

WO95/2066/3

The Naval & Military Press Ltd
www.nmarchive.com
Published in association with The National Archives

Published by

The Naval & Military Press Ltd

Unit 10 Ridgewood Industrial Park,

Uckfield, East Sussex,

TN22 5QE England

Tel: +44 (0) 1825 749494

www.naval-military-press.com

www.nmarchive.com

This diary has been reprinted in facsimile from the original. Any imperfections are inevitably reproduced and the quality may fall short of modern type and cartographic standards.

© **Crown Copyright**
Images reproduced by permission of The National Archives, London, England, 2015.

Contents

Document type	Place/Title	Date From	Date To
Heading	WO95/2066 Jly 1915-Nov 1918 ADVS-Part Of June Missing 1918		
Heading	19th Division A.D.V.S. Jly 1915-Nov 1918		
Heading	19th Division H.Q. 19th Div. A.D.V.S. Vol 2 Jly To Oct 15		
War Diary		16/07/1915	19/07/1915
War Diary	Tilques	20/07/1915	23/07/1915
War Diary	Hillaire	24/07/1915	24/07/1915
War Diary	Busnes	25/07/1915	30/07/1915
War Diary	Merville	31/07/1915	31/07/1915
War Diary	Merville	01/08/1915	30/08/1915
War Diary	Locon	31/08/1915	02/10/1915
War Diary	Fosse	03/10/1915	18/10/1915
War Diary	Locon	21/10/1915	31/10/1915
Heading	H.Q. 19th Div: A.D.V.S. Vol. 3 121/7656 Nov. 15		
War Diary	Locon	01/11/1915	23/11/1915
War Diary	St Venant	24/11/1915	30/11/1915
Heading	A.D.V.S. 19th Div: Vol: 4 Dec 1915		
War Diary	St Venant	01/12/1915	04/12/1915
War Diary	Lestrem	05/12/1915	31/12/1915
Heading	A.D.V.S. 19th Div: Vol: 5 Jan 16.		
War Diary	Lestrem	01/01/1916	24/01/1916
War Diary	St Venant	25/01/1916	31/01/1916
War Diary	St Venant	01/02/1916	16/02/1916
War Diary	La Gorgue	17/02/1916	29/02/1916
Heading	D.A.D.V.S. 19th. Divn. July 1915 To Nov. 1918		
War Diary		16/07/1915	19/07/1915
War Diary	Tilques	20/07/1915	23/07/1915
War Diary	Hillaire	24/07/1915	24/07/1915
War Diary	Busnes	25/07/1915	30/07/1915
War Diary	Merville	31/07/1915	31/07/1915
War Diary	Merville	01/08/1915	30/08/1915
War Diary	Locon	31/08/1915	02/10/1915
War Diary	Fosse	03/10/1915	18/10/1915
War Diary	Locon	21/10/1915	23/11/1915
War Diary	St Venant	24/11/1915	04/12/1915
War Diary	Lestrem	05/12/1915	24/01/1916
War Diary	St Venant	25/01/1916	16/02/1916
War Diary	La Gorgue	17/02/1916	31/03/1916
War Diary	La Gorgue	17/03/1916	17/04/1916
War Diary	St Venant	18/04/1916	19/04/1916
War Diary	Norrent Fontes	20/04/1916	30/04/1916
War Diary	La Gorgue	01/04/1916	17/04/1916
War Diary	St. Venant	18/04/1916	19/04/1916
War Diary	Norrent Fontes	20/04/1916	07/05/1916
War Diary	Flesselles	08/05/1916	31/05/1916
War Diary	La Gorgue	01/05/1916	17/05/1916
War Diary	St Venant	18/05/1916	19/05/1916
War Diary	Norrent Fontes	20/05/1916	30/05/1916
War Diary	Flesselles	01/06/1916	15/06/1916

War Diary	St Gratien	16/06/1916	30/06/1916
War Diary	Flesselles	01/06/1916	15/06/1916
War Diary	St Gratien	16/06/1916	30/06/1916
War Diary	Millencourt	01/07/1916	12/07/1916
War Diary	Henencourt	13/07/1916	20/07/1916
War Diary	Albert	21/07/1916	31/07/1916
War Diary	Millencourt	01/07/1916	12/07/1916
War Diary	Henencourt	13/07/1916	20/07/1916
War Diary	Albert	21/07/1916	31/07/1916
War Diary	Baizieux	01/08/1916	03/08/1916
War Diary	Long	04/08/1916	06/08/1916
War Diary	St Jans Cappel	07/08/1916	07/08/1916
War Diary	Westoutre	08/08/1916	31/08/1916
War Diary	Baizieux	01/08/1916	03/08/1916
War Diary	Long	04/08/1916	06/08/1916
War Diary	St Jans Cappel	07/08/1916	07/08/1916
War Diary	Westoutre	08/08/1916	06/09/1916
War Diary	Bailleul	07/09/1916	20/09/1916
War Diary	Merris	21/09/1916	30/09/1916
War Diary	Westoutre	01/09/1916	06/09/1916
War Diary	Bailleul	07/09/1916	20/09/1916
War Diary	Merris	21/09/1916	05/10/1916
War Diary	Marieux	06/10/1916	07/10/1916
War Diary	Authie	08/10/1916	17/10/1916
War Diary	Merris	01/10/1916	05/10/1916
War Diary	Marieux	06/10/1916	07/10/1916
War Diary	Authie	08/10/1916	17/10/1916
War Diary	Rubempre	18/10/1916	21/10/1916
War Diary	Warloy	22/10/1916	23/10/1916
War Diary	Bouzincourt	24/10/1916	31/10/1916
War Diary	Rubempre	18/10/1916	21/10/1916
War Diary	Warloy	22/10/1916	23/10/1916
War Diary	Bouzincourt	24/10/1916	22/11/1916
War Diary	Contay	23/11/1916	23/11/1916
War Diary	Doullens	24/11/1916	24/11/1916
War Diary	Bernaville	25/11/1916	30/11/1916
Miscellaneous	A.D.V.S.		
War Diary	Bouzincourt	01/11/1916	22/11/1916
War Diary	Contay	23/11/1916	23/11/1916
War Diary	Doullens	24/11/1916	24/11/1916
War Diary	Bernaville	25/11/1916	31/12/1916
War Diary	Bernaville	01/12/1916	09/01/1917
War Diary	Marieux	10/01/1917	11/01/1917
War Diary	Couin	12/01/1917	31/01/1917
War Diary	Bernaville	01/01/1917	09/01/1917
War Diary	Marieux	10/01/1917	11/01/1917
War Diary	Couin	12/01/1917	28/02/1917
War Diary	Couin	01/02/1917	04/03/1917
War Diary	Bus Les Artois	05/03/1917	10/03/1917
War Diary	Beauval	11/03/1917	11/03/1917
War Diary	Boquemaison	12/03/1917	13/03/1917
War Diary	Ramecourt	14/03/1917	14/03/1917
War Diary	Pernes	15/03/1917	16/03/1917
War Diary	Norrent Fontes	17/03/1917	18/03/1917
War Diary	Steenbecque	19/03/1917	19/03/1917
War Diary	Merris	20/03/1917	20/03/1917

War Diary	Fletre		21/03/1917	31/03/1917
War Diary	Couin		01/03/1917	04/03/1917
War Diary	Bus Les Artois		05/03/1917	10/03/1917
War Diary	Beauval		11/03/1917	11/03/1917
War Diary	Boquemaison		12/03/1917	13/03/1917
War Diary	Ramecourt		14/03/1917	14/03/1917
War Diary	Pernes		15/03/1917	16/03/1917
War Diary	Norrent Fontes		17/03/1917	18/03/1917
War Diary	Steenbecque		19/03/1917	19/03/1917
War Diary	Merris		20/03/1917	20/03/1917
War Diary	Fletre		21/03/1917	31/03/1917
War Diary	Westoutre		01/04/1917	30/04/1917
War Diary	Westoutre		01/04/1917	02/05/1917
War Diary	Busseboom		03/05/1917	12/05/1917
War Diary	Westoutre		13/05/1917	31/05/1917
War Diary	Westoutre		01/05/1917	02/05/1917
War Diary	Busseboom		03/05/1917	12/05/1917
War Diary	Westoutre		13/05/1917	19/06/1917
War Diary	St Jan's Cappel		20/06/1917	30/06/1917
War Diary	Westoutre		01/06/1917	19/06/1917
War Diary	St Jan's Cappel		20/06/1917	03/07/1917
War Diary	Scherpenberg		04/07/1917	31/07/1917
War Diary	St Jan's Cappell		01/07/1917	03/07/1917
War Diary	Scherpenberg		04/07/1917	08/08/1917
War Diary	St Jan's Cappel		09/08/1917	10/08/1917
War Diary	Lumbres		11/08/1917	29/08/1917
War Diary	St Jans Cappel		30/08/1917	31/08/1917
War Diary	Scherpenberg		01/08/1917	08/08/1917
War Diary	St Jan's Cappel		09/08/1917	10/08/1917
War Diary	Lumbres		11/08/1917	29/08/1917
War Diary	St Jans Cappel		30/08/1917	31/08/1917
War Diary	St Jan's Cappel		01/09/1917	12/09/1917
War Diary	Scherpenberg		13/09/1917	27/09/1917
War Diary	St Jan's Cappel		01/09/1917	12/09/1917
War Diary	Scherpenberg		13/09/1917	31/10/1917
War Diary	Scherpenberg		01/10/1917	09/11/1917
War Diary	St Jans Capel		10/11/1917	11/11/1917
War Diary	Blaringhem		12/11/1917	30/11/1917
War Diary	Scherpenberg		01/11/1917	09/11/1917
War Diary	St Jans Capel		10/11/1917	11/11/1917
War Diary	Blaringhem		12/11/1917	13/12/1917
War Diary	Meuville		14/12/1917	14/12/1917
War Diary	Bourjonval		15/12/1917	16/12/1917
War Diary	Meuville		17/12/1917	17/12/1917
War Diary	Bourjonval		18/12/1917	31/12/1917
War Diary	Blaringhem		01/12/1917	13/12/1917
War Diary	Meuville Bourjonval		14/12/1917	31/01/1918
War Diary	Meuville Bourjonval		01/01/1918	22/02/1918
War Diary	Haplincourt		23/02/1918	28/02/1918
War Diary	Meuville Bourjonval		01/02/1918	23/02/1918
War Diary	Haphicourt		23/02/1918	28/02/1918
War Diary	Meuville Bourjonval		01/02/1918	22/02/1918
War Diary	Haplincourt		23/02/1918	29/03/1918
War Diary	Dranoutre		30/03/1918	31/03/1918
War Diary	Haplincourt		01/03/1918	29/03/1918
War Diary	Dranoutre		30/03/1918	02/04/1918

War Diary	Stovel Camp		03/04/1918	10/04/1918
War Diary	Dranoutre		11/04/1918	11/04/1918
War Diary	Mont Noir		12/04/1918	13/04/1918
War Diary	Westoutre		14/04/1918	17/04/1918
War Diary	Abeele (Aerodrome)		18/04/1918	21/04/1918
War Diary	Provey		22/04/1918	29/04/1918
War Diary	L.13. Central (Sheet 27)		30/04/1918	30/04/1918
War Diary	Dranoutre		01/04/1918	02/04/1918
War Diary	Shavel Camp		03/04/1918	10/04/1918
War Diary	Dranoutre		11/04/1918	11/04/1918
War Diary	Mont Noir		12/04/1918	13/04/1918
War Diary	Westoutre		14/04/1918	17/04/1918
War Diary	Abeele (Aerodrome)		18/04/1918	21/04/1918
War Diary	Provey		22/04/1918	29/04/1918
War Diary	L.13. Central. (Sheet 27)		30/04/1918	13/05/1918
War Diary	Bambecque		14/05/1918	18/05/1918
War Diary	St Germain La Ville		19/05/1918	31/05/1918
War Diary	L.13. Central (Sheet 27)		01/05/1918	13/05/1918
War Diary	Bambecque		14/05/1918	18/05/1918
War Diary	St Germain La Ville		19/05/1918	31/05/1918
War Diary	Luis		13/06/1918	21/06/1918
War Diary	Mondement		22/06/1918	30/06/1918
War Diary	Luis		13/06/1918	21/06/1918
War Diary	Mondement		22/06/1918	02/07/1918
War Diary	Fauquembergues		03/07/1918	12/07/1918
War Diary	Bomy		13/07/1918	31/07/1918
War Diary	Maudewent		01/07/1918	02/07/1918
War Diary	Fauquembergues		03/07/1918	12/07/1918
War Diary	Bomy		13/07/1918	07/08/1918
War Diary	Labeuvriere		08/08/1918	31/08/1918
War Diary	Bomy		01/08/1918	08/08/1918
War Diary	Labeuvriere		09/08/1918	06/09/1918
War Diary	Bethune		07/09/1918	30/09/1918
War Diary	Labeuvriere		01/09/1918	06/09/1918
War Diary	Bethune		07/09/1918	03/10/1918
War Diary	Auchel Hewe		04/10/1918	08/10/1918
War Diary	Graincourt		09/10/1918	09/10/1918
War Diary	Mayelles		10/10/1918	13/10/1918
War Diary	Cambrai		14/10/1918	18/10/1918
War Diary	Avesues-Lez-Aubert		19/10/1918	20/10/1918
War Diary	St Aubert		21/10/1918	23/10/1918
War Diary	Avesues-Lez-Aubert		24/10/1918	31/10/1918
War Diary	Bethune		01/10/1918	03/10/1918
War Diary	Auchel		04/10/1918	04/10/1918
War Diary	Henu		05/10/1918	08/10/1918
War Diary	Graincourt		09/10/1918	09/10/1918
War Diary	Mayelles		10/10/1918	13/10/1918
War Diary	Cambrai		14/10/1918	18/10/1918
War Diary	Aubert Lez-Aubert		19/10/1918	20/10/1918
War Diary	St Aubert		21/10/1918	23/10/1918
War Diary	Avesues-Lez-Aubert		24/10/1918	03/11/1918
War Diary	Vendegies		04/11/1918	04/11/1918
War Diary	Sepmeries		05/11/1918	05/11/1918
War Diary	Jenlain		06/11/1918	08/11/1918
War Diary	La Flamengrie		09/11/1918	10/11/1918
War Diary	Wargnies Le Petit		11/11/1918	14/11/1918

War Diary	Vendegies	15/11/1918	15/11/1918
War Diary	Rieux	16/11/1918	25/11/1918
War Diary	Cambrai	26/11/1918	28/11/1918
War Diary	Naours	29/11/1918	30/11/1918
War Diary	Avesues-Lez-Aubert	01/11/1918	03/11/1918
War Diary	Vendegies	04/11/1918	04/11/1918
War Diary	Sepmeries	05/11/1918	05/11/1918
War Diary	Jenlain	06/11/1918	08/11/1918
War Diary	La Flamengrie	09/11/1918	10/11/1918
War Diary	Wargnies-Le-Petit	11/11/1918	14/11/1918
War Diary	Vendelles	15/11/1918	15/11/1918
War Diary	Rieux	16/11/1918	25/11/1918
War Diary	Cambrai	26/11/1918	28/11/1918
War Diary	Naours	29/11/1918	30/11/1918

WO 95
2066

July 1915 – Nov 1918
ADVS

— Part of June Missing 1918

19TH DIVISION

A. D. V. S.
JLY 1915 - NOV 1916

121/7432

19th Division

H.Q. 19th Div: ADMS.
Vol 2
Feb to Oct 15

Army Form C.2118

WAR DIARY

A.D.V.S., 19th Division.

Instructions regarding War Diaries and Intelligence Summaries are contained in F.S. Regs., Part II. and the Staff Manual respectively. Title Pages will be prepared in manuscript.

Place	Date 1915.	Hour	Summary of Events and Information	Remarks and References to Appendices
	July.			
	16.		Embarked at SOUTHAMPTON.	
	18.		Disembarked at HAVRE.	
	19.		En route to ST OMER.	
TILQUES.	20.		Arrived TILQUES via ST OMER.	
	21.		Headquarters in Distillery. Routine work.	
	22.		No. 31 M.V. Section arrived. Strength of Divn. Horses 4,437, Mules 1,337.	
	23.		Inspection of various units.	
HILLAIRE.	24.		Left TILQUES, arrived HILLAIRE.	
BUSNES?	25.		Moved to BUSNES. M.V.S. also moved.	
	26.		D.D.V.S., 1st Army called and inspected M.V.S.	
	27.		Inspected animals of D.H.Q., Signal Coy., and Ambulances.	
	28.		Inspection of animals of Infy. Bdes.	
	29.		D.D.V.S., 1st Army called. Strength Horses 4,389, Mules 1,336.	
	30.		Routine work. Inspected M.V.S. Very difficult to secure float for removal of sick or injured animals even on payment of hire of float, which is five francs.	
MERVILLE.	31.		Moved to MERVILLE. Office in private house at No. 20 Rue de Bethune.	

WAR DIARY of A.D.V.S., 19th Division.

INTELLIGENCE SUMMARY

(Erase heading not required.)

Army Form C.2118

Instructions regarding War Diaries and Intelligence Summaries are contained in F.S. Regs., Part II. and the Staff Manual respectively. Title Pages will be prepared in manuscript.

Place	Date 1915. Aug.	Hour	Summary of Events and Information	Remarks and references to Appendices
MERVILLE	1.		Inspected 82nd Field Coy. R.E.	
	2.		Inspected D.H.Q., and Signal Company. No. 7510, L/Crpl. Wilson evacuated to Base Hospital.	
	3.		Routine work.	
	4.		Inspected D.A.C. and Field Ambulances.	
	5.		D.D.V.S., called. Strength 4351, mules 1360.	
	6.		Inspected 81st Field Company, R.E., C Battery, 89th Bde. R.F.A., attached Lahore Division.	
	7.		Routine work. B/89th Bde. R.F.A. transferred.	
	8.		Inspected D.H.Q., and Signal Company.	
	9.		To HASBROUCK.	
HASBROUCK	10.		Inspected M.V.S.	
	11.		Inspected D.H.Q., and Signal Company.	
	12.		To Remount Depot, GONNEHEM. Strength 4186 horses, 1318 mules.	
	13.		Routine Work.	
	14.		Inspected M.V.S., D.H.Q., and Signal Company.	
	15.		Inspected D/87th Bde, R.F.A.,	
	16.		Routine work. Directed that all suspected skin disease cases be sent to M.V.S. with man on foot.	
	17.		Inspected 81st and 82nd Field Coys. R.E.	

-1-

Army Form C. 2118

WAR DIARY of A.D.V.S., 19th Division.

INTELLIGENCE SUMMARY

(Erase heading not required.)

Instructions regarding War Diaries and Intelligence Summaries are contained in F. S. Regs., Part II. and the Staff Manual respectively. Title Pages will be prepared in manuscript.

Place	Date 1915.	Hour	Summary of Events and Information	Remarks and references to Appendices
MERVILLE	Aug. 18.		Inspected 88th B.A.C., R.F.A.	
	19th		Inspected D.H.Q., and Signal Company. Strength, horses 4150, mules 1328.	
	20.		To GONNEHEM. Selected 3 chargers for Veterinary Officers.	
	21.		D.D.V.S., (Lt-Col. A.C.Newsom) called and visited M.V.S. to see Lance Corporals, A.V.C. with Infy. Bdes. re promotion to Sergeants.	
	22.		Inspected M.V.S. Very hard to get floats herefor removal of sick horses. Hire of float 5 francs.	
	23.		Routine work.	
	24.		Routine work. Inspected D.H.Q., and Signal Company.	
	25.		Routine work. No. 7510, L/Crpl. Wilson returned to duty. Issued Smoke Helmets for horses to Units at rate of 10% of total strength.	
	26.		Routine work and Inspections.	
	27.		To LOCON to locate billets for M.V.S.	
	28.		Inspected D.A.C. Strength, horses 4183, mules 1329.	
	29.		Routine work.	
	30.		Routine work. Notified D.D.V.S. that Lieut. A.R.Smythe's agreement terminated 31st instant.	
LOCON.	31.		Moved to LOCON.	

1875 Wt. W593/826 1,000,000 4/15 J.B.C. & A. A.D.S.S./Forms/C. 2118.

Army Form C. 2118

WAR DIARY of A.D.V.S., 19th Division.

INTELLIGENCE SUMMARY

(Erase heading not required.)

Instructions regarding War Diaries and Intelligence Summaries are contained in F.S. Regs., Part II. and the Staff Manual respectively. Title Pages will be prepared in manuscript.

Place	Date	Hour	Summary of Events and Information	Remarks and references to Appendices
LOCON.	1915. Septr.			
	1.		Routine work.	
	2.		All V.O's reported. Strength, horses 4193, mules 1327.	
	3.		Routine inspections.	
	4.		Routine inspections. No 6547, Pte. Murrell, M.V.S., died in hospital of Pneumonia. Conference of A.D.'s V.S. at ESTAIRES.	
	5.		Inspections and routine work.	
	6.		Inspected D.H.Q. and Signal Company.	
	7.		Routine work.	
	8.		Routine work. D.D.V.S. called.	
	9.		Routine work. Strength, horses 4215, mules 1335.	
	10.		Routine work and inspections.	
	11.		Routine work.	
	12.		Routine work. Received A.F. B 122 of 3 sergeants A.V.C. posted to 19th Division.	
	13.		Inserted in Divisional Orders that heel shackles must be used when picketing.	
	14.		Routine work.	
	15.		Inspected various units.	
	16.		All V.O's reported. Strength, horses 4183, mules 1507.	
	17.		Inspected D.H.Q. and Signal Company.	

Army Form C. 2118

WAR DIARY of A.D.V.S., 19th Division.

INTELLIGENCE SUMMARY

(Erase heading not required.)

Instructions regarding War Diaries and Intelligence Summaries are contained in F. S. Regs., Part II. and the Staff Manual respectively. Title Pages will be prepared in manuscript.

Place	Date	Hour	Summary of Events and Information	Remarks and references to Appendices
	1915. Septr			
LOCON.	18.		Inspected Divl. Train, A.S.C.	
	19.		Inspected M.V.S.	
	20.		To LE FACONS, to select place for Advanced Collecting Station.	
	21.		Established Advanced Collecting Station at LE FACONS. Heavy Artillery bombardment.	
	22.		Inspection of Units. Bombardment continued. Raining.	
	23		Bombardment continued. D.D.V.S. called. Raining. Strength, horses 4188, mules 1321.	
	24.		All V.O's reported.	
	25.		Inspection. Visited Advanced Collecting Station. Raining.	
	26.		Inspections. D.D.V.S. called. Weather fine.	
	27.		Routine work.	
	28.		Inspected D.H.Q., and 19th Signal Coy. Took over Veterinary charge of Sirhind Brigade attached.	
	29.		Inspections. 58th Infy. Brigade temporarily detached to 7th Division.	
	30.		Inspections. Strength, horses 4328, mules 1206. Float for moving horses has to be obtained from BETHUNE. Cannot always be obtained when required.	

Army Form C. 2118

WAR DIARY of A.D.V.S., 19th Division;

~~INTELLIGENCE SUMMARY~~

(Erase heading not required.)

Instructions regarding War Diaries and Intelligence Summaries are contained in F.S. Regs., Part II. and the Staff Manual respectively. Title Pages will be prepared in manuscript.

Place	Date 1915	Hour	Summary of Events and Information	Remarks and references to Appendices
LOCON.	Octr. 1.		All V.O's reported.	
	2.		Routine work.	
FOSSE.	3.		Departed LOCON. Arrived Fosse. Took over Veterinary charge of 2nd London Heavy and 13th Heavy Batteries of 17th Heavy Brigade, R.G.A.	
	4.		To LOCON to see A.D.V.S., Meerut Division.	
	5.		Inspected 2nd London Heavy and 13th Heavy Batteries with Lieut. W. A. McGill, A.V.C. A/89th Brigade attached Meerut Division.	
	6.		Inspected M.V.S. and other Units. 58th Infy. Bde. rejoined 19th Division.	
	7.		Inspected R.A. Strength, horses 4416, mules 1314.	
	8.		All V.O's reported. O.C. 17th Heavy Brigade reported Lieut. McGill, A.V.C. under arrest. Telegraphed D.D.V.S. who called at 3.0.p.m.	
	9.		Routine work. D.D.V.S. called at 11.30.a.m.	
	10.		Routine work.	
	11.		Routine work. D.D.V.S. called and visited O.C., 17th Heavy Brigade.	
	12.		Routine work. Inspected M.V.S., afternoon.	
	13.		Inspections.	
	14.		Inspected D.H.Q. Strength, horses 4444, mules 1340.	
	15.		All V.O's reported. No float suitable for removing horses available. Horses frequently have to wait several days for means of transportation.	

-1-

Army Form C. 2118

WAR DIARY of A.D.V.S., 19th Division.

INTELLIGENCE SUMMARY

(Erase heading not required.)

Instructions regarding War Diaries and Intelligence Summaries are contained in F.S. Regs., Part II. and the Staff Manual respectively. Title Pages will be prepared in manuscript.

Place	Date 1915	Hour	Summary of Events and Information	Remarks and references to Appendices
FOSSE.	Oct r 16.		Inspected 81st Field Company, R.E.	
	17.		Inspected M.V.S.	
	18.		Special Leave granted to A.D.V.S.,for purposes of proceeding to Ireland on important private business, by G.O.C., 19th Division. Captain H.Bone, A.V.C., 31st.M.V.S., took over duties.	
LOCON.	21.		Arrived LOCON.	
	28.		A.D.V.S. returned from leave. Strength, horses 4195, mules 1320.	
	29.		All V.O's reported.	
	30.		Conference of A.D's V.S. held at M.V.S. D.D.V.S. present.	
	31.		Inspections of Units and routine work.	

HD. 19 to Brig: ADVS.
Vol. 3

121/7656

Nov. 15

Army Form C. 2118

WAR DIARY of A.D.V.S., 19th Division.

or INTELLIGENCE SUMMARY

(Erase heading not required.)

Instructions regarding War Diaries and Intelligence Summaries are contained in F.S. Regs., Part II. and the Staff Manual respectively. Title Pages will be prepared in manuscript.

Place	Date	Hour	Summary of Events and Information	Remarks and references to Appendices
LOCON.	Nov. 1st.		Inspections M.V.S. Heavy rain.	
"	2nd.		Inspections Signal Coy and Divisional Headquarters. Heavy rain.	
"	3rd.		D.D.V.S. 1st Army called - Routine work.	
"	4th.		Inspections a.m. - Capt. H. Bone, A.V.C., O.C.31st M.V.S. left on leave - Strength, Horses 4204, Mules 1332.	
"	5th.		All V.Os reported - Received instructions from D.D.V.S. to exchange two men with M. V. S., Meerut Division. Transferred two men to Meerut Division.	
"	6th.		Inspections and Routine work.	
"	7th.		Inspections and Routine work.	
"	8th.		Inspected D.A.C. - Routine work.	
"	9th.		Inspected Divisional Headquarters and Signals. - Routine work.	
"	10th.		Inspected all Companies R. E.	
"	11th.		Inspected new standings of Signal Coy. Strength, Horses 4443, Mules 874.	
"	12th.		All V.Os reported. D.D.V.S. called.	
"	13th.		Instruction in Intra-dermal Palpebral method of Malleinization at M.V.S. by D.D.V.S. Capt. H. Bone returned from leave.	
"	14th.		Lieut-Colonel A. C. Newsom and Lieut-Colonel E. E. Martin (appointed D.D.V.S. 1st Army) called. Routine work.	
"	15th.		Inspected Divisional Headquarters and Signals.	
"	16th.		Inspected Infantry Brigades.	

J.S. Moore Major, A.V.C., A.D.V.S., 19th Division.

Army Form C. 2118

WAR DIARY of A.D.V.S., 19th Division.

INTELLIGENCE SUMMARY

(Erase heading not required.)

Instructions regarding War Diaries and Intelligence Summaries are contained in F.S. Regs., Part II. and the Staff Manual respectively. Title Pages will be prepared in manuscript.

Place	Date	Hour	Summary of Events and Information	Remarks and references to Appendices
LOCON.	Nov. 17th.		Inspected Divisional Train. - Difficult to secure floats for moving sick animals. Closest at BETHUNE property of Knecker. Hire 5 frs.	
	" 18th.		Routine work and Inspections. - Capt. A. R. Smythe, A.V.C., i/c 56th, 57th, 58th Infantry Brigades and 5th South Wales Borderers, went on leave. - Strength, Horses 4410, Mules 830.	
	" 19th.		All V.Os reported. - Routine work.	
	" 20th.		Inspections a.m. - Afternoon to AIRE.	
	" 21st.		Inspections. - Went to FOSSE to see A.D.V.S., 46th Division, re occupation of billets of M.V.S.	
	" 22nd.		Routine work. - Inspected Signal Coy and Divisional Headquarters.	
	" 23rd.		Routine work. - Inspected D.A.C.	
ST VENANT.	" 24th.		Moved to ST VENANT and occupied room on RUE DE PAS DE CALAIS as Office.	
	" 25th.		To ROBECQ to inspect animals of Units stationed there. - Strength, Horses 4449, Mules 858. No float here - nearest at MERVILLE - very uncertain when it can be obtained.	
	" 26th.		All V.Os reported. - Inspected M.V.S. at LE HAYE.	
	" 27th.		Inspected 88th Brigade, R.F.A. at BAS HAMEL.	
	" 28th.		To AIRE to see D.D.V.S. - Capt. A. R. Smythe returned from leave.	
	" 29th.		D.D.V.S. called and inspected M.V.S. - Lieut J. M. Brown, A.V.C., i/c 86th, and 87th Brigades, R.F.A. on leave.	
	" 30th.		Inspected 56th, 57th, and 58th Infantry Brigades. - A.D.V.S., 46th Division called.	

Jas. Miller, Major, A.V.C.,
A.D.V.S., 19th Division.

Akts. og b. dir.
Vol. 4

121/7910

Nov 19/15

Army Form C. 2118

WAR DIARY of A.D.V.S., 19th Division.
or
INTELLIGENCE SUMMARY

(Erase heading not required.)

Instructions regarding War Diaries and Intelligence Summaries are contained in F.S. Regs., Part II. and the Staff Manual respectively. Title Pages will be prepared in manuscript.

Place	Date 1915	Hour	Summary of Events and Information	Remarks and references to Appendices
ST VENANT.	Dec 1st.		Inspection of M.V.S. Weather clear.	fasm.
"	2nd.		Inspection and Routine Work. Cloudy. Strength, Horses 4620, Mules 854.	fasm.
"	3rd.		All V.Os reported. Rain.	fasm.
"	4th.		To LOCON and FOSSE to inspect billets for M.V.S. Collecting stations. Weather clear.	fasm.
LESTREM.	5th.		Moved to LESTREM - M.V.S. to PARADIS. Clear.	fasm.
	6th.		Inspections and Routine. Showers.	fasm.
	7th.		Inspections and Routine. A.D.V.S. Guards Division called. Showers.	fasm.
	8th.		To LOCON, FOSSE, and LOCOUTURE to inspect units there. Showers.	fasm.
	9th.		Inspections. Weather clear. Strength, Horses 6197, Mules 769.	fasm.
	10th.		All V.Os called. Routine work. Clear.	fasm.
	11th.		M.V.S. malleined. Light Showers.	fasm.
	12th.		One reaction reported at M.V.S. Reported fact personally to D.D.V.S., 1st Army in AIRE. Clear	fasm.
	13th.		D.D.V.S., 1st Army called with syringes and mallein and inspected reactor at M.V.S. Reactor charger of A.D.V.S.	fasm.
	14th.		Lieut Kerr, A.V.C. left on leave. D.D.V.S. called. Weather clear.	fasm.
	15th.		D.D.V.S. called and visited M.V.S. Reactor destroyed. Post Mortem held. Started to test other units of Division beginning with 86th Brigade R.F.A. Clear.	fasm.
	16th.		Inspections and routine. Weather clear. Strength, Horses 6215, Mules 764.	fasm.

fasshoo, Major. A.V.C.

Army Form C. 2118

WAR DIARY
or
INTELLIGENCE SUMMARY

(Erase heading not required.)

of A.D.V.S., 19th Division.

Instructions regarding War Diaries and Intelligence Summaries are contained in F.S. Regs., Part II. and the Staff Manual respectively. Title Pages will be prepared in manuscript.

Place	Date 1915.	Hour	Summary of Events and Information	Remarks and references to Appendices
LESTREM.	Dec 17th.		All V.Os reported. Weather clear.	Fair.
"	18th.		Malleined all animals 19th Signal Coy.	Fall.
"	19th.		Inspected Signal Coy - no reactions. Clear.	Fair.
"	20th.		Inspected Signal Coy and 86th Brigade R.F.A. Clear.	Fresh.
"	21st.		Inspections and routine. Clear.	Fair.
"	22nd.		Inspections and Routine. Showers.	Fair.
"	23rd.		Inspections and Routine. Light showers. Strength, Horses 6221, Mules 770.	Fair.
"	24th.		Inspections and Routine. All V.Os reported. Lieut Kerr returned from leave. Clear.	Fair.
"	25th.		Inspections and Routine. Clear.	Fair.
"	26th.		Inspections and Routine. Clear.	Fair.
"	27th.		Inspections and Routine. Clear.	Fair.
"	28th.		Inspected two reported doubtful reactions at M.V.S. Notified D.D.V.S. Lieut T. Menzies left on leave. Cloudy.	Fair.
"	29th.		Retested cases at M.V.S. Clear.	Fair.
"	30th.		Reactions at M.V.S doubtful - to be retested. Strength, Horses 6848, Mules 789. Cloudy.	Fair.
"	31st.		All V.Os reported. Inspections and Routine. Clear.	Fair.

Major. A.V.C.

Army Form C. 2118

WAR DIARY of A.D.V.S., 19th Division.

INTELLIGENCE SUMMARY

(Erase heading not required.)

Instructions regarding War Diaries and Intelligence Summaries are contained in F.S. Regs., Part II. and the Staff Manual respectively. Title Pages will be prepared in manuscript.

Place	Date 1916.	Hour	Summary of Events and Information	Remarks and references to Appendices
LESTREM	Jany. 1st		Inspections and routine work. Weather clear.	Fasu.
	2nd.		Inspected 31st Mobile Veterinary Section. Weather clear.	Fasu.
	3rd.		Inspected D.H.Q. and Signal Company. Weather cloudy.	Fasu.
	4th.		To M.V.S. Horse No. 31 of 35 H. Bde., R.G.A. destroyed as reactor to Mallein Test. Took over Veterinary charge of 113th Inf. Bde. and No. 331 Coy., A.S.C. Weather cloudy.	Fasu. Fasu.
	5th		Inspections and routine work. Weather cloudy.	Fasu.
	6th.		Inspections and routine work. Weather cloudy. Strength, horses 6192, mules 795.	Fasu.
	7th.		All Veterinary Officers reported at Office. Weather clear.	Fasu.
	8th.		Inspected Divisional Train, A.S.C. Lieut. T. Menzies, A.V.C., returned from leave. Weather clear.	Fasu.
	9th.		To AIRE. Weather cloudy.	Fasu.
	10th.		Inspected D.A.C. remounts. Lieut. Walpole, A.V.C., left on leave. Weather cloudy.	Fasu.
	11th.		D.D.V.S., 1st Army called and inspected M.V.S. Weather clear.	Fasu.
	12th.		Inspected D.A.C. Weather clear.	Fasu.
	13th.		Inspected Infy. Bdes. Weather clear.	Fasu.
	14th.		Inspections and routine work. Strength, horses 5668, mules 923. Weather clear.	Fasu.
	15th.		All Veterinary Officers reported. Inspected Divisional Train. Inspected 89th Bde. R.F.A. Took over Vety. charge of D/121st Brigade, R.F.A. Weather clear.	Fasu.
	16th.		Inspected M.V.S. Routine work.	Fasu.

-1-

Army Form C. 2118

WAR DIARY
~~INTELLIGENCE SUMMARY~~ of A.D.V.S., 19th Division.
(Erase heading not required.)

Instructions regarding War Diaries and Intelligence Summaries are contained in F.S. Regs., Part II. and the Staff Manual respectively. Title Pages will be prepared in manuscript.

Place	Date 1916.	Hour	Summary of Events and Information	Remarks and references to Appendices
LESTREM.	17th.		Inspected D.H.Q. Took over Vety. charge of 151st Field Coy. R.E. Raining.	F.a.s.U.
	18th.		Inspected Signal Company. Transferred No. 3602, Sgt. B. Eggleton to Guards D.A.C. Raining.	F.a.s.U.
	19th.		Inspected 86th Bde. R.F.A. Weather cloudy.	F.a.s.U.
	20th.		To GONNEHEM. (Field Remounts). Strength, horses 5756, mules 924. Weather cloudy.	F.a.s.U.
	21st.		All Veterinary Officers reported. Weather clear.	F.a.s.U.
	22nd.		Inspections and routine work. Weather clear.	F.a.s.U.
	23rd.		Inspections and routine work. To M.V.S. Weather clear.	F.a.s.U.
	24th.		D.H.Q. moved to St. VENANT. Inspected D.A.C. with D.D.R. and D.D.V.S. Weather clear.	F.a.s.U.
St VENANT.	25th.		Inspections and routine work. Weather cloudy.	F.a.s.U.
	26th.		Inspections and routine work. Weather cloudy.	F.a.s.U.
	27th.		M.V.S. moved to LA HAYE. Strength, horses 4682 mules 876. Weather cloudy.	F.a.s.U.
	28th.		All Veterinary Officers reported. Routine work. Weather clear.	F.a.s.U.
	29th.		Inspections and routine work. Weather clear.	F.a.s.U.
	30th.		To AIRE. Routine work. Weather cloudy and foggy.	F.a.s.U.
	31st.		Inspection of M.V.S. Routine work. Weather cloudy.	F.a.s.U.

Lashlun Major
A.r.C.
A.D.V.S. 19 Division

-2-

Army Form C. 2118

WAR DIARY A.D.V.S., 19th Division.
INTELLIGENCE SUMMARY
(Erase heading not required.)

Instructions regarding War Diaries and Intelligence Summaries are contained in F. S. Regs., Part II. and the Staff Manual respectively. Title Pages will be prepared in manuscript.

Place	Date 1916.	Hour	Summary of Events and Information	Remarks and references to Appendices
ST VENANT.	Feb. 1.		Inspections and routine work. Weather cloudy.	F.a.S.M.
	2.		Inspected D.H.Q. and 19th Divl. Signal Company. Weather cloudy.	F.a.S.M.
	3.		Inspected Infantry Brigades. Strength, horses 4508, mules 856. Weather cloudy.	F.a.S.M.
	4.		Inspected Mobile Veterinary Section. All Veterinary Officers reported. F.Q.M.S. Fitzgerald transferred to No. 2 Veterinary Hospital. Weather cloudy.	F.a.S.M.
	5.		Inspections and routine work. Weather clear.	F.a.S.M.
	6.		To AIRE. Routine work. Weather cloudy.	F.a.S.M.
	7.		Inspections and Routine work. Weather cloudy.	F.a.S.M.
	8.		Inspected 86th Bde. R.F.A. Ordered 12 horses to be evacuated for debility. Weather cloudy.	F.a.S.M.
	9.		Inspected 87th Bde. R.F.A. Raining.	F.a.S.M.
	10.		Routine work and to M.V.S. Strength, horses 4535 horses, mules, 949. Raining.	F.a.S.M.
	11.		Inspected R.E. All Veterinary Officers reported. Raining.	F.a.S.M.
	12.		Inspected Divisional Train, A.S.C., Ordered 10 horses to be evacuated for debility. Weather cloudy.	F.a.S.M.
	13.		Inspected various units. Weather cloudy.	F.a.S.M.
	14.		Inspections and routine work. Weather clear.	F.a.S.M.
	15.		Inspected Mobile Veterinary Section's billets at LA GORGUE. Weather clear.	F.a.S.M.
	16.		Inspections and routine work. Raining.	F.a.S.M.

Army Form C. 2118

WAR DIARY
or
INTELLIGENCE SUMMARY 19th Division.
(Erase heading not required.)

Instructions regarding War Diaries and Intelligence Summaries are contained in F. S. Regs., Part II. and the Staff Manual respectively. Title Pages will be prepared in manuscript.

Place	Date	Hour	Summary of Events and Information	Remarks and references to Appendices
LA GORGUE	1916. Feb. 17.		Moved to LA GORGUE. Office at Rue de la Gare. Took over Veterinary charge of 11th Corps H.Q., Corps Signal Section, H.Q., Heavy Artillery Group, 255 Coy. R.E., 145 Coy. (Army Troops) R.E., 1st Army Aux. (Transport) Coy. A.S.C., and Labour Corps. Strength, horses 4853, Mules 1112. Weather clear.	L a S M.
	18.		Conference of Veterinary Officers at Office. In afternoon D.D.V.S., 1st Army called. Weather cloudy.	L a S M.
	19.		Inspected O.O., and Y.Y. Sections Corps Cable Section. 31st Mobile Veterinary Section moved to billets north of LA GORGUE. Weather clear.	L a S M.
	20.		Inspected various attached units. Lieut. T.H. Sherlock, A.V.C., reported for duty. Weather cloudy.	L a S M. L a S M.
	21.		Attended Field General Court Martial on C.Q.M.S. Perrott, 19th Divisional Train, A.S.C. Lieut. H. Walpole, A.V.C., left for England on expiration of contract. Weather clear.	L a S M.
	22.		Left on leave for England. Captain H. Bone, A.V.C., acting as A.D.V.S. Snowing.	
	23.		On leave.	
	24.		"	Jas. Moon M/Col
	25.		"	A.D.V.S
	26.		"	19H Division
	27.		"	
	28.		"	
	29.		"	

1875. Wt. W593/826 1,000,000 4/15 J.B.C. & A. A.D.S/Forms/C. 2118.

DADY'S   DUPL

19th Divn

July 1915
to
Nov. 1918

Army Form C. 2118

WAR DIARY A.D.V.S., 19th Division.

INTELLIGENCE SUMMARY

(Erase heading not required.)

Instructions regarding War Diaries and Intelligence Summaries are contained in F.S. Regs., Part II. and the Staff Manual respectively. Title Pages will be prepared in manuscript.

Place	Date 1915. July.	Hour	Summary of Events and Information	Remarks and references to Appendices
	16.		Embarked at SOUTHAMPTON.	
	18.		Disembarked at HAVRE.	
	19.		En route to ST OMER.	
TILQUES.	20.		Arrived TILQUES via ST OMER.	
	21.		Headquarters in Distillery. Routine work.	
	22.		No. 31 M.V. Section arrived. Strength of Divn. Horses 4,437, Mules 1,337.	
	23.		Inspection of various units.	
HILLAIRE.	24.		Left TILQUES, arrived HILLAIRE.	
BUSNES?	25.		Moved to BUSNES. M.V.S. also moved.	
	26.		D.D.V.S., 1st Army called and inspected M.V.S.	
	27.		Inspected animals of D.H.Q., Signal Coy., and Ambulances.	
	28.		Inspection of animals of Infy. Bdes.	
	29.		D.D.V.S., 1st Army called. Strength Horses 4,389, Mules 1,336.	
	30.		Routine work. Inspected M.V.S. Very difficult to secure float for removal of sick or injured animals even on payment of hire of float, which is five francs.	
MERVILLE.	31.		Moved to MERVILLE. Office in private house at No. 20 Rue de Bethune.	

Army Form C. 2118

WAR DIARY of A.D.V.S., 19th Division.

~~INTELLIGENCE SUMMARY~~

(Erase heading not required.)

Instructions regarding War Diaries and Intelligence Summaries are contained in F. S. Regs., Part II. and the Staff Manual respectively. Title Pages will be prepared in manuscript.

Place	Date	Hour	Summary of Events and Information	Remarks and references to Appendices
	1915. Aug.			
MERVILLE	1.		Inspected 82nd Field Coy. R.E.	
	2.		Inspected D.H.Q., and Signal Company. No. 7510, L/Crpl. Wilson evacuated to Base Hospital.	
	3.		Routine work.	
	4.		Inspected D.A.C. and Field Ambulances.	
	5.		D.D.V.S., called. Strength 4351, mules 1360.	
	6.		Inspected 81st Field Company, R.E., C Battery, 89th Bde. R.F.A., attached Lahore Division.	
	7.		Routine work. B/89th Bde. R.F.A. transferred.	
	8.		Inspected D.H.Q., and Signal Company.	
	9.		To HASBROUCK.	
	10.		Inspected M.V.S.	
	11.		Inspected D.H.Q., and Signal Company.	
	12.		To Remount Depot, GONNEHEM. Strength 4186 horses, 1318 mules.	
	13.		Routine Work.	
	14.		Inspected M.V.S., D.H.Q., and Signal Company.	
	15.		Inspected D/87th Bde, R.F.A.,	
	16.		Routine work. Directed that all suspected skin disease cases be sent to M.V.S. with man on foot.	
	17.		Inspected 81st and 82nd Field Coys R.E.	

—1—

Army Form C. 2118

WAR DIARY of A.D.V.S., 19th Division.

INTELLIGENCE SUMMARY

(Erase heading not required.)

Instructions regarding War Diaries and Intelligence Summaries are contained in F.S. Regs., Part II. and the Staff Manual respectively. Title Pages will be prepared in manuscript.

Place	Date 1915.	Hour	Summary of Events and Information	Remarks and references to Appendices
MERVILLE	Aug. 18.		Inspected 88th B.A.C., R.F.A.	
	19th		Inspected D.H.Q., and Signal Company. Strength, horses 4150, mules 1328.	
	20		To GONNEHEM. Selected 3 chargers for Veterinary Officers.	
	21.		D.D.V.S., (Lt-Col. A.C.Newsom) called and visited M.V.S. to see Lance Corporals, A.V.C. with Infy. Bdes. re promotion to Sergeants.	
	22.		Inspected M.V.S. Very hard to get floats herefor removal of sick horses. Hire of float 5 francs.	
	23.		Routine work.	
	24.		Routine work. Inspected D.H.Q., and Signal Company.	
	25.		Routine work. No. 7510, L/Crpl. Wilson returned to duty. Issued Smoke Helmets for horses to Units at rate of 10% of total strength.	
	26.		Routine work and Inspections.	
	27.		To LOCON to locate billets for M.V.S.	
	28.		Inspected D.A.C. Strength, horses 4183, mules 1329.	
	29.		Routine work.	
	30.		Routine work. Notified D.D.V.S. that Lieut. A.R.Smythe's agreement terminated 31st instant.	
LOCON.	31.		Moved to LOCON.	

Army Form C. 2118

WAR DIARY of A.D.V.S., 19th Division.
INTELLIGENCE SUMMARY
(Erase heading not required.)

Instructions regarding War Diaries and Intelligence Summaries are contained in F. S. Regs., Part II. and the Staff Manual respectively. Title Pages will be prepared in manuscript.

Place	Date	Hour	Summary of Events and Information	Remarks and references to Appendices
LOCON.	1915. Septr.			
	1.		Routine work.	
	2		All V.O's reported. Strength, horses 4193, mules 1327.	
	3.		Routine inspections.	
	4		Routine inspections. No 6547, Pte. Murrell, M.V.S., died in hospital of Pneumonia. Conference of A.D's V.S. at ESTAIRES.	
	5		Inspections and routine work.	
	6.		Inspected D.H.Q. and Signal Company.	
	7		Routine work.	
	8		Routine work. D.D.V.S. called.	
	9		Routine work. Strength, horses 4215, mules 1335.	
	10.		Routine work and inspections.	
	11.		Routine work.	
	12.		Routine work. Received A.F. B 122 of 3 sergeants A.V.C. posted to 19th Division.	
	13.		Inserted in Divisional Orders that heel shackles must be used when picketing.	
	14.		Routine work.	
	15.		Inspected various units.	
	16.		All V.O's reported. Strength, horses 4183, mules 1307.	
	17.		Inspected D.H.Q. and J Signal Coy.	

Army Form C. 2118

WAR DIARY of A.D.V.S., 19th Division.

INTELLIGENCE SUMMARY

(Erase heading not required.)

Instructions regarding War Diaries and Intelligence Summaries are contained in F. S. Regs., Part II. and the Staff Manual respectively. Title Pages will be prepared in manuscript.

Place	Date	Hour	Summary of Events and Information	Remarks and references to Appendices
	1915. Sept.			
LOCON.	18.		Inspected Divl. Train, A.S.C.	
	19.		Inspected M.V.S.	
	20.		To LE FACONS, to select place for Advanced Collecting Station.	
	21.		Established Advanced Collecting Station at LE FACONS. Heavy Artillery bombardment.	
	22.		Inspection of Units. Bombardment continued. Raining.	
	23.		Bombardment continued. D.D.V.S. called. Raining. Strength, horses 4188, mules 1321.	
	24.		All V.O's reported.	
	25.		Inspection. Visited Advanced Collecting Station. Raining.	
	26.		Inspections. D.D.V.S. called. Weather fine.	
	27.		Routine Work.	
	28.		Inspected D.H.Q., and 19th Signal Coy. Took over Veterinary charge of Sirhind Brigade attached.	
	29.		Inspections. 58th Infy. Brigade temporarily detached to 7th Division.	
	30.		Inspections. Strength, horses 4323, mules 1206. Float for moving horses has to be obtained from BETHUNE. Cannot always be obtained when required.	Jas Moore A.D.V.S. A.D.V.S. 19th Division.

Army Form C. 2118

WAR DIARY of A.D.V.S., 19th Division;
INTELLIGENCE SUMMARY
(Erase heading not required.)

Instructions regarding War Diaries and Intelligence Summaries are contained in F.S. Regs., Part II. and the Staff Manual respectively. Title Pages will be prepared in manuscript.

Place	Date 1915 Octr.	Hour	Summary of Events and Information	Remarks and references to Appendices
LOCON.	1.		All V.O's reported.	
	2.		Routine work.	
FOSSE.	3.		Departed LOCON. Arrived Fosse. Took over Veterinary charge of 2nd London Heavy and 13th Heavy Batteries of 17th Heavy Brigade, R.G.A.	
	4.		To LOCON to see A.D.V.S., Meerut Division.	
	5.		Inspected 2nd London Heavy and 13th Heavy Batteries with Lieut. W. A. McGill, A.V.C. A/89th Brigade attached Meerut Division.	
	6.		Inspected M.V.S. and other Units. 58th Infy. Bde. rejoined 19th Division.	
	7.		Inspected R.A. Strength, horses 4416, mules 1314.	
	8.		All V.O's reported. O.C. 17th Heavy Brigade reported Lieut. McGill, A.V.C. under arrest. Telegraphed D.D.V.S. who called at 3.0.p.m. D.D.V.S. called at 11.30.a.m.	
	9.		Routine work.	
	10.		Routine work.	
	11.		Routine work. D.D.V.S. called and visited O.C., 17th Heavy Brigade.	
	12.		Routine work. Inspected M.V.S., afternoon.	
	13.		Inspections.	
	14.		Inspected D.H.Q. Strength, horses 4444, mules 1340.	
	15.		All V.O's reported. No float suitable for removing horses available. Horses frequently have to wait several days for means of transportation.	

—1—

Army Form C. 2118

WAR DIARY of A.D.V.S., 19th Division.

INTELLIGENCE SUMMARY

(Erase heading not required.)

Place	Date	Hour	Summary of Events and Information	Remarks and references to Appendices
	1915. Oct.			
FOSSE.	16.		Inspected 81st Field Company, R.E.	
	17.		Inspected M.V.S.	
	18.		Special Leave granted to A.D.V.S., for purposes of proceeding to Ireland on important private business, by G.O.C., 19th Division. Captain H.Bone, A.V.C., 31st M.V.S., took over duties.	
LOCON.	21.		Arrived LOCON.	
	28.		A.D.V.S. returned from leave. Strength, horses 4195, mules 1320.	
	29.		All V.O's reported.	
	30.		Conference of A.D's V.S. held at M.V.S. D.D.V.S. present.	
	31.		Inspections of Units and routine work.	

Army Form C. 2118

WAR DIARY of A.D.V.S., 19th Division.
or
INTELLIGENCE SUMMARY
(Erase heading not required.)

Instructions regarding War Diaries and Intelligence Summaries are contained in F.S. Regs., Part II. and the Staff Manual respectively. Title Pages will be prepared in manuscript.

Place	Date	Hour	Summary of Events and Information	Remarks and references to Appendices
LOCON.	Nov.1st.		Inspections M.V.S. Heavy rain.	
"	2nd.		Inspections Signal Coy and Divisional Headquarters. Heavy rain.	
"	3rd.		D.D.V.S. 1st Army called - Routine work.	
"	4th.		Inspections a.m. - Capt. H. Bone, A.V.C., O.C.31st M.V.S. left on leave - Strength, Horses 4204, Mules 1332.	
"	5th.		All V.Os reported - Received instructions from D.D.V.S. to exchange two men with M. V. S., Meerut Division. Transferred two men to Meerut Division.	
"	6th.		Inspections and Routine work.	
"	7th.		Inspections and Routine work.	
"	8th.		Inspected D.A.C. - Routine work.	
"	9th.		Inspected Divisional Headquarters and Signals. - Routine work.	
"	10th.		Inspected all Companies R. E.	
"	11th.		Inspected new standings of Signal Coy. Strength, Horses 4443, Mules 874.	
"	12th.		All V.Os reported. D.D.V.S. called.	
"	13th.		Instruction in Intra-dermal Palpebral method of Malleinization at M.V.S. by D.D.V.S. Capt. H. Bone returned from leave.	
"	14th.		Lieut-Colonel A. C. Newsom and Lieut-Colonel E. E. Martin (appointed D.D.V.S. 1st Army) called. Routine work.	
"	15th.		Inspected Divisional Headquarters and Signals.	
"	16th.		Inspected Infantry Brigades.	

Major, A.V.C., A.D.V.S., 19th Division.

Army Form C. 2118

WAR DIARY of A.D.V.S., 19th Division.
or
INTELLIGENCE SUMMARY
(Erase heading not required.)

Instructions regarding War Diaries and Intelligence Summaries are contained in F. S. Regs., Part II. and the Staff Manual respectively. Title Pages will be prepared in manuscript.

Place	Date	Hour	Summary of Events and Information	Remarks and references to Appendices
LOCON.	Nov. 17th.		Inspected Divisional Train. - Difficult to secure floats for moving sick animals. Closest at BETHUNE property of Knecker. Hire 5 frs.	
"	18th.		Routine work and Inspections. - Capt. A. R. Smythe, A.V.C., i/c 56th, 57th, 58th Infantry Brigades and 5th South Wales Borderers, went on leave. - Strength, Horses 4410, Mules 830.	
"	19th.		All V.Os reported. - Routine work.	
"	20th.		Inspections a.m. - Afternoon to AIRE.	
"	21st.		Inspections. - Went to FOSSE to see A.D.V.S., 46th Division, re occupation of billets of M.V.S.	
"	22nd.		Routine work. - Inspected Signal Coy and Divisional Headquarters.	
"	23rd.		Routine work. - Inspected D.A.C.	
ST VENANT.	24th.		Moved to ST VENANT and occupied room on RUE DE PAS DE CALAIS as Office.	
"	25th.		To ROBECQ to inspect animals of Units stationed there. - Strength, Horses 4449, Mules 858.	
"	26th.		No float here - nearest at MERVILLE - very uncertain when it can be obtained. All V.Os reported. - Inspected M.V.S. at LE HAYE.	
"	27th.		Inspected 88th Brigade, R.F.A. at EAS HAMEL.	
"	28th.		To AIRE to see D.D.V.S. - Capt. A. R. Smythe returned from leave.	
"	29th.		D.D.V.S. called and inspected M.V.S. - Lieut J. M. Brown, A.V.C., i/c 86th, and 87th Brigades, R.F.A. on leave.	
"	30th.		Inspected 56th, 57th, and 58th Infantry Brigades. - A.D.V.S., 46th Division called.	

Jas Major, A. V. C.,
A. D. V. S., 19th Division.

Army Form C. 2118

WAR DIARY of A.D.V.S., 19th Division.
or
INTELLIGENCE SUMMARY
(Erase heading not required.)

Instructions regarding War Diaries and Intelligence Summaries are contained in F.S. Regs., Part II. and the Staff Manual respectively. Title Pages will be prepared in manuscript.

Place	Date 1915.	Hour	Summary of Events and Information	Remarks and references to Appendices
ST VENANT.	Dec 1st.		Inspection of M.V.S. Weather clear.	fair.
"	2nd.		Inspection and Routine Work. Cloudy. Strength, Horses 4620, Mules 854.	fair.
"	3rd.		All V.Os reported. Rain.	fair.
"	4th.		To LOCON and FOSSE to inspect billets for M.V.S.Collecting stations. Weather clear.	fair.
LESTREM.	5th.		Moved to LESTREM - M.V.S. to PARADIS. Clear.	fair.
"	6th.		Inspections and Routine. Showers.	fair.
"	7th.		Inspections and Routine. A.D.V.S. Guards Division called. Showers.	fair.
"	8th.		To LOCON, FOSSE, and LOCOUTURE to inspect units there. Showers.	fair.
"	9th.		Inspections. Weather clear. Strength, Horses 6197, Mules 769.	fair.
"	10th.		All V.Os called. Routine work. Clear.	fair.
"	11th.		M.V.S. malleined. Light Showers.	fair.
"	12th.		One reaction reported at M.V.S. Reported fact personally to D.D.V.S., 1st Army in AIRE. Clear	fair.
"	13th.		D.D.V.S., 1st Army called with syringes and mallein and inspected reactor at M.V.S. Reactor charger of A.D.V.S.	fair.
"	14th.		Lieut Kerr, A.V.C. left on leave. D.D.V.S. called. Weather clear.	fair.
"	15th.		D.D.V.S. called and visited M.V.S. Reactor destroyed. Post Mortem held. Started to test other units of Division beginning with 86th Brigade R.F.A. Clear.	fair.
"	16th.		Inspections and routine. Weather clear. Strength, Horses 6215, Mules 764.	fair.

Major. A.V.C.

Army Form C. 2118

WAR DIARY of A.D.V.S., 19th Division.
or
INTELLIGENCE SUMMARY
(Erase heading not required.)

Instructions regarding War Diaries and Intelligence Summaries are contained in F.S. Regs., Part II. and the Staff Manual respectively. Title Pages will be prepared in manuscript.

Place	Date 1915.	Hour	Summary of Events and Information	Remarks and references to Appendices
LESTREM	Dec 17th.		All V.Os reported. Weather clear.	fum.
"	18th.		Malleined all animals 19th Signal Coy. Clear.	fum.
"	19th.		Inspected Signal Coy - no reactions. Clear.	fum.
"	20th.		Inspected Signal Coy and 86th Brigade R.F.A. Clear.	fum.
"	21st.		Inspections and routine. Clear.	fum.
"	22nd.		Inspections and Routine. Showers.	fum.
"	23rd.		Inspections and Routine. Light showers. Strength, Horses 6221, Mules 770.	fum.
"	24th.		Inspections and Routine. All V.Os reported. Lieut Kerr returned from leave. Clear.	fum.
"	25th.		Inspections and Routine. Clear.	fum.
"	26th.		Inspections and Routine. Clear.	fum.
"	27th.		Inspections and Routine. Clear.	fum.
"	28th.		Inspected two reported doubtful reactions at M.V.S. Notified D.D.V.S. Lieut T. Menzies left on leave. Cloudy.	fum.
"	29th.		Retested cases at M.V.S. Clear.	fum.
"	30th.		Reactions at M.V.S doubtful - to be retested. Strength, Horses 6848, Mules 789. Cloudy.	fum.
"	31st.		All V.Os reported. Inspections and Routine. Clear.	fum.

Major. A.V.C.

Army Form C. 2118

WAR DIARY

of A.D.V.S., 19th Division.

INTELLIGENCE SUMMARY

(Erase heading not required.)

Place	Date 1916	Hour	Summary of Events and Information	Remarks and references to Appendices
LESTREM.	Jany. 1st		Inspections and routine work. Weather clear.	F a s u
	2nd.		Inspected 31st Mobile Veterinary Section. Weather clear.	F a s u
	3rd.		Inspected D.H.Q. and Signal Company. Weather cloudy.	F a s u
	4th.		To M.V.S. Horse No. 31 of 35 H. Bde., R.G.A. destroyed as reactor to Mallein Test. Took over Veterinary charge of 113th Inf. Bde. and No. 331 Coy., A.S.C. Weather cloudy.	F a s u
	5th.		Inspections and routine work. Weather cloudy.	F a s u
	6th.		Inspections and routine work. Weather cloudy. Strength, horses 6192, mules 795.	F a s u
	7th.		All Veterinary Officers reported at Office. Weather clear.	F a s u
	8th.		Inspected Divisional Train, A.S.C. Lieut. T. Menzies, A.V.C., returned from leave. Weather clear.	F a s u
	9th.		To AIRE. Weather cloudy.	F a s u
	10th.		Inspected D.A.C. remounts. Lieut. Walpole, A.V.C., left on leave. Weather cloudy.	F a s u
	11th.		D.D.V.S., 1st Army called and inspected M.V.S. Weather clear.	F a s u
	12th.		Inspected D.A.C. Weather clear.	F a s u
	13th.		Inspected Infy. Bdes. Weather clear.	F a s u
	14th.		Inspections and routine work. Strength, horses 5668, mules 923. Weather clear.	F a s u
	15th.		All Veterinary Officers reported. Inspected Divisional Train. Inspected 89th Bde. R.F.A. Took over Vety. charge of D/121st Brigade, R.F.A. Weather clear.	F a s u
	16th.		Inspected M.V.S. Routine work.	F a s u

Jas Moore Major
A.D.V.S.
A D V S 19 Division

Army Form C. 2118

WAR DIARY
or
INTELLIGENCE SUMMARY

of A.D.V.S., 19th Division.

(Erase heading not required.)

Instructions regarding War Diaries and Intelligence Summaries are contained in F.S. Regs., Part II. and the Staff Manual respectively. Title Pages will be prepared in manuscript.

Place	Date 1916.	Hour	Summary of Events and Information	Remarks and references to Appendices
LESTREM.	17th.		Inspected D.H.Q. Took over Vety. charge of 151st Field Coy. R.E. Raining.	$\mathcal{L}$ as M.
	18th.		Inspected Signal Company. Transferred No. 3602, Sgt. B. Eggleton to Guards D.A.C. Raining.	$\mathcal{L}$ as M.
	19th.		Inspected 86th Bde. R.F.A. Weather cloudy.	$\mathcal{L}$ as M.
	20th.		To GONNEHEM. (Field Remounts). Strength, horses 5756, mules 924. Weather cloudy.	$\mathcal{L}$ as M.
	21st.		All Veterinary Officers reported. Weather clear.	$\mathcal{L}$ as M.
	22nd.		Inspections and routine work. weather clear.	$\mathcal{L}$ as M.
	23rd.		Inspections and routine work. To M.V.S. Weather clear.	$\mathcal{L}$ as M.
	24th.		D.H.Q. moved to St. VENANT. Inspected D.A.C. with D.D.R. and D.D.V.S. Weather clear.	$\mathcal{L}$ as M.
St VENANT.	25th.		Inspections and routine work. Weather cloudy.	$\mathcal{L}$ as M.
	26th.		Inspections and routine work. Weather cloudy.	$\mathcal{L}$ as M.
	27th.		M.V.S. moved to LA HAYE. Strength, horses 4682 mules 876. Weather cloudy.	$\mathcal{L}$ as M.
	28th.		All Veterinary Officers reported. Routine work. Weather clear.	$\mathcal{L}$ as M.
	29th.		Inspections and routine work. Weather clear.	$\mathcal{L}$ as M.
	30th.		To AIRE. Routine work. Weather cloudy and foggy.	$\mathcal{L}$ as M.
	31st.		Inspection of M.V.S. Routine work. Weather cloudy.	$\mathcal{L}$ as M.

-2-

Lasdovic Major
A.D.V.S 19 Division

Army Form C. 2118

WAR DIARY of INTELLIGENCE SUMMARY

A.D.V.S., 19th Division.

(Erase heading not required.)

Instructions regarding War Diaries and Intelligence Summaries are contained in F.S. Regs., Part II. and the Staff Manual respectively. Title Pages will be prepared in manuscript.

Place	Date 1916.	Hour	Summary of Events and Information	Remarks and references to Appendices
ST VENANT.	Feb. 1.		Inspections and routine work. Weather cloudy.	F.4.S.M.
	2.		Inspected D.H.Q. and 19th Divl. Signal Company. Weather cloudy.	F.2.S.M.
	3.		Inspected Infantry Brigades. Strength, horses 4508, mules 856. Weather cloudy.	F.2.S.M.
	4.		Inspected Mobile Veterinary Section. All Veterinary Officers reported. F.Q.M.S. Fitzgerald transferred to No. 2 Veterinary Hospital. Weather cloudy.	F.2.S.M.
	5.		Inspections and routine work. Weather clear.	F.2.S.M.
	6.		To AIRE. Routine work. Weather cloudy.	F.2.S.M.
	7.		Inspections and Routine work. Weather cloudy.	F.2.S.M.
	8.		Inspected 86th Bde. R.F.A. Ordered 12 horses to be evacuated for debility. Weather cloudy.	F.2.6.M.
	9.		Inspected 87th Bde. R.F.A. Raining.	F.2.S.M.
	10.		Routine work and to M.V.S. Strength, horses 4535, mules, 949. Raining.	F.2.S.M.
	11.		Inspected R.E. All Veterinary Officers reported. Raining.	F.2.6.M.
	12.		Inspected Divisional Train, A.S.C., Ordered 10 horses to be evacuated for debility. Weather cloudy.	F.4.S.M.
	13.		Inspected various units. Weather cloudy.	F.2.S.M.
	14.		Inspections and routine work. Weather clear.	F.2.S.M.
	15.		Inspected Mobile Veterinary Section's billets at LA GORGUE. Weather clear.	F.2.S.M.
	16.		Inspections and routine work. Raining.	F.2.S.M.

-1-

Army Form C. 2118

WAR DIARY

INTELLIGENCE SUMMARY of A.D.V.S., 19th Division.

(Erase heading not required.)

Instructions regarding War Diaries and Intelligence Summaries are contained in F.S. Regs., Part II. and the Staff Manual respectively. Title Pages will be prepared in manuscript.

Place	Date 1916. Feb.	Hour	Summary of Events and Information	Remarks and references to Appendices
LA GORGUE	17.		Moved to LA GORGUE. Office at Rue de la Gare. Took over Veterinary charge of 11th Corps H.Q., Corps Signal Section, H.Q., Heavy Artillery Group, 255 Coy. R.E., 145 Coy. (Army Troops) R.E., 1st Army Aux. (Transport) Coy. A.S.C., and Labour Corps. Strength, horses 4853, Mules 1112. Weather clear.	I.a.S.M. I.a.S.M. I.a.S.M.
	18.		Conference of Veterinary Officers at Office. In afternoon D.D.V.S., 1st Army called. Weather cloudy.	I.a.S.M.
	19.		Inspected O., O.O., and Y.Y. Sections Corps Cable Section. 31st Mobile Veterinary Section moved to billets north of LA GORGUE. Weather clear.	I.a.S.M.
	20.		Inspected various attached units. Lieut. T.H. Sherlock, A.V.C., reported for duty. Weather cloudy.	I.a.S.M. I.a.S.M. I.a.S.M.
	21.		Attended Field General Court Martial on C.Q.M.S. Perrott, 19th Divisional Train, A.S.C. Lieut. H. Walpole, A.V.C., left for England on expiration of contract. Weather clear.	
	22.		Left on leave for England. Captain H. Bone, A.V.C., acting as A.D.V.S. Snowing.	
	23.		On leave.	
	24.		"	I.a.S. Moore Major
	25.		"	A.D.V.S.
	26.		"	19th Division
	27.		"	
	28.		"	
	29.		"	

-2-

Army Form C. 2118

WAR DIARY
of A.D.V.S.
INTELLIGENCE SUMMARY. 19th Division.
(Erase heading not required.)

Place	Date Hour	Summary of Events and Information	Remarks and references to Appendices
LA GORGUE.	1913. March 1.	On leave. Capt. H. Bone, A.V.C., Acting A.D.V.S.	
	2.	-do- -do-	
	3.	-do- -do-	
	4.	Returned from leave.	
	5.	Routine work and inspected M.V.S.	
	6.	Routine work and inspected 19th Signal Coy. and D.H.Q.	
	7.	Inspections. Reported deficiency of one A.V.C. Sergeant with D.A.C. to replace No. 32217, P.Q.M.S. Underwood, evacuated.	
	8.	Inspected D/86th Brigade, R.F.A. and A/86th Brigade R.F.A.	
	9.	Inspected 5th South Wales Borderers. Took over Veterinary charge of 166th Inf. Bde. and No. 4 Coy. A.S.C. (55th Division).	
	10.	All Veterinary Officers reported at Office.	
	11.	Inspections and routine work.	
	12.	To AIRE to see D.D.V.S., First Army.	
	13.	Inspected B/87th Brigade Ammunition Column, R.F.A.	
	14.	Inspected Divisional Train, A.S.C., and A/88th Brigade, R.F.A.	
	15.	Inspected 86th Brigade Ammunition Column, R.F.A.	
	16.	Inspected 253rd Tunnelling Company, R.E.	

Army Form C. 2118

WAR DIARY

INTELLIGENCE SUMMARY
19th Division.

Place	Date 1916.	Hour	Summary of Events and Information	Remarks and references to Appendices
LA GORGUE.	March 17.		All Veterinary Officers reported. Forwarded A.F. A 200 of 146th Inf. Bde. and No. 4 Coy. A.S.C. to A.D.V.S., 55th Division, these units leaving this Division.	
	18.		Inspected 7/East Lancs. Regt. and Divisional Ammunition Column.	
	19.		Routine work. Forwarded to D.D.V.S., second agreement of Lieutenant T.E.Sherlock, A.V.C., recommended for re-engagement.	
	20.		Inspected D.A.C.	
	21.		Routine work. Captain H. Bone, A.V.C., left for England on leave.	
	22.		Inspected Divisional Signal Company.	
	23.		Inspected Divisional Train.	
	24.		All Veterinary Officers reported. A.D.V.S., 8th Division called.	
	25.		Inspected 81st and 94th Field Coys. R.E.	
	26.		Routine work and inspected M.V.S.	
	27.		Inspected 57th Brigade Machine Gun Section and 255th Tunnelling Coy., R.E.	
	28.		Routine work and inspections of various units.	
	29a		Inspected 19th Signal Company, D/86th Bde. R.F.A., and A/86th Bde. R.F.A.	
	30.		Inspected 87th Brigade Ammunition Column, B/86th Bde. R.F.A., A/86th Brigade, R.F.A.	
	31.		All Nurse Veterinary Officers reported. ********	
			The weather during the early part of the month was cold, with snow and rain; during the middle of the month, unsettled; the latter part much warmer and generally clear.	

-2-

Army Form C. 2118

WAR DIARY
of A.D.V.S.
INTELLIGENCE SUMMARY. 19th Division.
(Erase heading not required.)

Instructions regarding War Diaries and Intelligence Summaries are contained in F.S. Regs., Part II. and the Staff Manual respectively. Title Pages will be prepared in manuscript.

Place	Date 1916.	Hour	Summary of Events and Information	Remarks and references to Appendices
LA GORGUE.	March 17.		All Veterinary Officers reported. Forwarded A.F. A 2000 of 106th Infy. Bde. and No. 4 Coy. A.S.C. to A.D.V.S., 35th Division, these units leaving this Division.	
	18.		Inspected 7/East Lancs. Regt. and Divisional Ammunition Column.	
	19.		Routine work. Forwarded to D.D.V.S., second agreement of Lieutenant T.H.Sherlock, A.V.C., recommended for re-engagement.	
	20.		Inspected D.A.C.	
	21.		Routine work. Captain H. Bone, A.V.C., left for England on leave.	
	22.		Inspected Divisional Signal Company.	
	23.		Inspected Divisional Train.	
	24.		All Veterinary Officers reported. A.D.V.S., 8th Division called.	
	25.		Inspected 81st and 94th Field Coys. R.E.	
	26.		Routine work and inspected M.V.S.	
	27.		Inspected 57th Brigade Machine Gun Section and 255th Tunnelling Coy. R.E.	
	28.		Routine work and inspections of various units.	
	29.		Inspected 19th Signal Company, D/86th Bde. R.F.A., and A/88th Bde. R.F.A.	
	30.		Inspected 87th Brigade Ammunition Column, B/86th Bde. R.F.A., A/86th Brigade, R.F.A.	
	31.		All Veter Veterinary Officers reported. **********	
			The weather during the early part of the month was cold, with snow and rain; during the middle very stormy, unsettled; thereafter part much warmer and generally clear.	

-2-

Army Form C. 2118

WAR DIARY
of A.D.V.S., 19th Division.

INTELLIGENCE SUMMARY

(Erase heading not required.)

Instructions regarding War Diaries and Intelligence Summaries are contained in F.S. Regs., Part II. and the Staff Manual respectively. Title Pages will be prepared in manuscript.

Place	Date 1916	Hour	Summary of Events and Information	Remarks and references to Appendices
Le GORGUE	1.		Routine work and inspected 56th Infy. Bde. and M.G. Coy.	Fau.
	2.		To D.D.V.S., First Army.	Fau.
	3.		Inspected D.A.C.	Fau.
	4.		Evacuated 28 animals to NEUFCHATEL. Capt. A.R.Smythe, A.V.C., left on leave.	Fau.
	5.		Inspected 81st Field Coy. R.E., 10th Worcester Regt., and A/89th Bde. R.F.A.	Fau.
	6.		Inspected Baggage Transport, Divisional Train.	Fau.
	7.		Weekly conference of Veterinary Officers. Inspected 19th Signal Coy. and D.H.Q.	Fau.
	8.		Examined chargers of G.O.C., 58th Infy. Bde.	Fau.
	9.		Evacuated 4 animals. Inspected 57th Bde. M.G.Coy.	Fau.
	10.		To D.D.V.S., First Army.	Fau.
	11.		Evacuated 20 animals. Inspected 8th Bn. North Staff. Regt.	Fau.
	12.		Routine work.	Fau.
	13.		Raining. Routine work and inspected D.H.Q.	Fau.
	14.		Weekly conference of Veterinary Officers. Inspected 6th Wilts. Regt.	Fau.
	15.		Inspected 19th Signal Coy.	Fau.
	16.		Routine work. Inspected Mobile Veterinary Section.	Fau.
	17.		Evacuated 36 animals. Routine work.	Fau.

-1-

Army Form C. 2118

WAR DIARY
of A.D.V.S., 19th Division.

~~INTELLIGENCE SUMMARY~~

(Erase heading not required.)

Instructions regarding War Diaries and Intelligence Summaries are contained in F. S. Regs., Part II. and the Staff Manual respectively. Title Pages will be prepared in manuscript.

Place	Date 1916	Hour	Summary of Events and Information	Remarks and references to Appendices
LA GORGUE.	May 17.		M.V.S. moved to LA HAYE. A.D.V.S! Office to St. VENANT. Inspected 86th Bde. A.C.	fasu.
				fasu.
ST. VENANT.	18.		Inspected 87th Bde. R.F.A., A.C. and D.A.C.	fasu.
	19.		Evacuated 45 animals. Moved to NORRENT FONTES. 14 animals evacuated.	fasu.
NORRENT FONTES.	20.		Routine work.	fasu.
	21.		Weekly conference of Veterinary Officers. M.V.S. moved to ST. HILAIRE.	fasu.
	22.		Inspected local units.	fasu.
	23.		Inspections and routine work.	fasu.
	24.		Inspected 81st Field Coy. R.E.	fasu.
	25.		13 animals evacuated. Inspected 82nd Field Coy. R.E.	fasu.
	26.		With D.D.V.S. and D.D.R. inspected 89th Bde. R.F.A.	fasu.
	27.		Inspections and routine work.	fasu.
	28.		Inspected 88th Bde. R.F.A. with D.D.V.S. and D.D.R. Weekly conference of Veterinary Officers. 39 animals evacuated.	fasu.
	29.		Inspected Divisional Train.	fasu.
	30.		Evacuated 44 animals. To LINGHEM to Competition of animals of 1st Line Transport. ******* During the early part of the month the weather was wet but towards the end extremely warm and fine. Between 23rd and 28th all Veterinary wallets in possession of A.V.C. Sergeants and Farriers were examined and deficiencies noted.	fasu.

-2-

Army Form C. 2118

89

WAR DIARY
of A.D.V.S., 19th Division.
INTELLIGENCE SUMMARY
(Erase heading not required.)

Instructions regarding War Diaries and Intelligence Summaries are contained in F. S. Regs., Part II. and the Staff Manual respectively. Title Pages will be prepared in manuscript.

Place	Date 1916.	Hour	Summary of Events and Information	Remarks and references to Appendices
Le GORGUE	1.		Routine work and inspected 56th Infy. Bde. and M.G. Coy.	Fair.
	2.		To D.D.V.S., First Army.	Fair.
	3.		Inspected D.A.C.	Fair.
	4.		Evacuated 28 animals to NEUFCHATEL. Capt. A.R.Smythe, A.V.C., left on leave. Inspected 81st Field Coy. R.E., 10th Worcester Regt., and A/89th Bde. R.F.A.	Fair.
	5.		Inspected Baggage Transport, Divisional Train.	Fair.
	6.		Weekly conference of Veterinary Officers. Inspected 19th Signal Coy. and D.H.Q.	Fair.
	7.		Examined chargers of G.O.C., 56th Infy. Bde.	Fair.
	8.		Evacuated 4 animals. Inspected 57th Bde. M.G.Coy.	Fair.
	9.		To D.D.V.S., First Army.	Fair.
	10.		Evacuated 20 animals. Inspected 8th Bn. North Staff. Regt.	Fair.
	11.		Routine work.	Fair.
	12.		Raining. Routine work and inspected D.H.Q.	Fair.
	13.		Weekly conference of Veterinary Officers. Inspected 8th Wilts. Regt.	Fair.
	14.		Inspected 19th Signal Coy.	Fair.
	15.		Routine work. Inspected Mobile Veterinary Section.	Fair.
	16.		Evacuated 36 animals. Routine work.	Fair.

Army Form C. 2118

WAR DIARY
of A.D.V.S., 19th Division.
INTELLIGENCE SUMMARY
(Erase heading not required.)

Instructions regarding War Diaries and Intelligence Summaries are contained in F.S. Regs., Part II. and the Staff Manual respectively. Title Pages will be prepared in manuscript.

Place	Date 1916	Hour	Summary of Events and Information	Remarks and references to Appendices
LA GORGUE.	May 17.		M.V.S. moved to LA HAYE. A.D.V.S. Office to St. VENANT. Inspected 88th Bde. A.C.	fair
ST. VENANT.	18.		Inspected 87th Bde. R.F.A., A.O. and D.A.C. 14 animals evacuated.	fair
	19.		Evacuated 45 animals. Moved to NORRENT FONTES.	fair
NORRENT FONTES.	20.		Routine work.	fair
	21.		Weekly conference of Veterinary Officers. M.V.S. moved to ST. HILAIRE.	fair
	22.		Inspected local units.	fair
	23.		Inspections and routine work.	fair
	24.		Inspected 81st Field Coy. R.E.	fair
	25.		13 animals evacuated. Inspected 82nd Field Coy. R.E.	fair
	26.		With D.D.V.S. and D.D.R. Inspected 89th Bde. R.F.A.	fair
	27.		Inspections and routine work.	fair
	28.		Inspected 88th Bde. R.F.A. with D.D.V.S. and D.D.R. Weekly conference of Veterinary Officers. 39 animals evacuated.	fair
	29.		Inspected Divisional Train.	fair
	30.		Evacuated 44 animals. To LINGHEM to Competition of animals of 1st Line Transport.	fair
			During the early part of the month the weather was wet but towards the end extremely warm and fine. Between 23rd and 28th all Veterinary wallets in possession of A.V.C. Sergeants and Farriers were examined and deficiencies noted.	fair fair

-2-

Eastman Major
A.D.V.S. 19 Divn.

Army Form C. 2118

WAR DIARY
or
INTELLIGENCE SUMMARY

19th Division.

Instructions regarding War Diaries and Intelligence Summaries are contained in F.S. Regs., Part II. and the Staff Manual respectively. Title Pages will be prepared in manuscript.

Place	Date	Hour	Summary of Events and Information	Remarks and references to Appendices
	1916. May.			
NORRENT FONTES.	1.		Evacuated 44 Animals to Base Hospital. Inspected 86th Bde. R.F.A.	F.a.S.M.
	2.		Evacuated 38 animals. Routine work.	F.a.S.M.
	3.		A.D.V.S., 38th Division called. Routine work.	F.a.S.M.
	4.		Evacuated 13 animals. Routine work.	F.a.S.M.
	5.		Weekly conference of Veterinary Officers. To AIRE to see D.D.V.S.	F.a.S.M.
	6.		Inspected 82nd Field Coy. R.E.	F.a.S.M.
	7.		D.H.Q. moved to FLESSELLES. Office at No. Rue d'Eustache, FLESSELLES.	F.a.S.M.
FLESSELLES	8.		Inspected 6th Wilts. and No. 3 Section Fourth Army Aux. H.T. Inspected site for Mobile Veterinary Section at ST VAST.	F.a.S.M.
	9.		Took over veterinary charge of Section Fourth Army A.H.T. Coy. at VIGNACOURT. Mobile Veterinary Section moved to ST. VAST.	F.a.S.M.
	10.		D.D.V.S., Fourth Army called. Routine work.	F.a.S.M.
	11.		Inspected 82nd Field Coy. R.E.	F.a.S.M.
	12.		Weekly conference of Veterinary Officers. Routine work.	F.a.S.M.
	13.		Inspections and routine work.	F.a.S.M.
	14.		Inspected 19th Divisional Train.	F.a.S.M.
	15.		All Officers' veterinary chests inspected at M.V.S. Inspected Signal Coy. Section at H.Q. R.A., at BELLOY.	F.a.S.M.

Army Form C. 2118

WAR DIARY or INTELLIGENCE SUMMARY

19th Division.

(Erase heading not required.)

Instructions regarding War Diaries and Intelligence Summaries are contained in F.S. Regs., Part II. and the Staff Manual respectively. Title Pages will be prepared in manuscript.

Place	Date 1916.	Hour	Summary of Events and Information	Remarks and references to Appendices
FLESSELLES	May 16.		Inspected 19th Divl. Signal Company.	Fasll.
	17.		Inspected 19th Divl. Signal Company.	Fasll.
	18.		Inspected 57th Infantry Brigade.	Fasll.
	19.		Weekly conference of Veterinary Officers. Captain Sherlock left on leave.	Fasll.
	20.		Inspected D.A.C.	Fasll.
	21.		Routine work. Inspected M.V.S. and D.H.Q.	Fasll.
	22.		Took over veterinary charge of one troop III Corps Cavalry Regiment. Inspected 58th Infy. Bde.	Fasll.
	23.		Inspected 56th Infantry Brigade.	Fasll.
	24.		Inspected D.A.C.	Fasll.
	25.		Inspected 58th Field Ambulance and 154 Coy. A.S.C.	Fasll.
	26.		Weekly conference of Veterinary Officers. Evacuated 48 animals.	Fasll.
	27.		Inspected M.V.S. Routine work.	Fasll.
	28.		Inspected units at VIGNACOURT.	Fasll.
	29.		57th and 58th Infy. Bdes. left for training area, also 88th Bde. R.F.A. Inspected 86th and 87th Bdes. R.F.A.	Fasll.
	30.		Routine work. Inspected M.V.S.	Fasll.
	31.		Fourth Army Aux. H.T. Coy. left Divl. area for ALBERT. The weather during the month has been generally fine.	Fasll.

Fasslooss Majote
A.D.V.S. 19 Division

Army Form C. 2118

WAR DIARY
or
INTELLIGENCE SUMMARY

of A.D.V.S., 19th Division.

Vol 8

(Erase heading not required.)

Place	Date 1916	Hour	Summary of Events and Information	Remarks and references to Appendices
Le GORGUE	May 1.		Routine Work and inspected 56th Infy. Bde. and M.G. Coy.	Fasll.
	2.		To D.D.V.S., First Army.	Fasll.
	3.		Inspected D.A.C.	Fasll.
	4.		Evacuated 28 animals to NEUFCHATEL. Capt. A.R.Smythe, A.V.C., left on leave. Inspected 81st Field Coy. R.E., 10th Worcester Regt., and A/89th Bde. R.F.A.	Fasll. Fasll.
	5.		Inspected Baggage Transport, Divisional Train.	Fasll.
	6.		Weekly conference of Veterinary Officers. Inspected 19th Signal Coy. and D.H.Q.	Fasll.
	7.		Examined chargers of G.O.C., 58th Infy. Bde.	Fasll.
	8.		Evacuated 4 animals. Inspected 57th Bde. M.G.Coy.	Fasll.
	9.		To D.D.V.S., First Army.	Fasll.
	10.		Evacuated 20 animals. Inspected 8th Bn. North Staff. Regt.	Fasll.
	11.		Routine work.	Fasll.
	12.		Raining. Routine work and inspected D.H.Q.	Fasll.
	13.		Weekly conference of Veterinary Officers. Inspected 6th Wilts. Regt.	Fasll.
	14.		Inspected 19th Signal Coy.	Fasll.
	15.		Routine work. Inspected Mobile Veterinary Section.	Fasll.
	16.		Evacuated 50 animals. Routine work.	Fasll.

Army Form C. 2118

WAR DIARY
or
INTELLIGENCE SUMMARY

A.D.V.S. 19th Division.

(Erase heading not required.)

Instructions regarding War Diaries and Intelligence Summaries are contained in F.S. Regs., Part II. and the Staff Manual respectively. Title Pages will be prepared in manuscript.

Place	Date	Hour	Summary of Events and Information	Remarks and references to Appendices
LA GORGUE.	1916. May. 17.		M.V.S. moved to LA HAYE. A.D.V.S? Office to St. VENANT. Inspected 86th Bde. A.C.	Fasu.
ST. VENANT.	18.		Inspected 87th Bde. R.F.A., A.C. and D.A.C. 14 animals evacuated.	Fasu.
	19.		Evacuated 45 animals. Moved to NORRENT FONTES.	Fasu.
NORRENT FONTES.	20.		Routine work.	Fasu.
	21.		Weekly conference of Veterinary Officers. M.V.S. moved to ST. HILAIRE.	Fasu.
	22.		Inspected local units.	Fasu.
	23.		Inspections and routine work.	Fasu.
	24.		Inspected 81st Field Coy. R.E.	Fasu.
	25.		13 animals evacuated. Inspected 82nd Field Coy. R.E.	Fasu.
	26.		With D.D.V.S. and D.D.R. Inspected 89th Bde. R.F.A.	Fasu.
	27.		Inspections and routine work.	Fasu.
	28.		Inspected 88th Bde. R.F.A. with D.D.V.S. and D.D.R. Weekly conference of Veterinary Officers. 39 animals evacuated.	Fasu.
	29.		Inspected Divisional Train.	Fasu.
	30.		Evacuated 44 animals. To LINGHEM to Competition of animals of 1st line Transport.	Fasu.
			******* During the early part of the month the weather was wet but towards the end extremely warm and fine. Between 23rd and 28th all Veterinary wallets in possession of A.V.C. Sergeants and Farriers were examined and deficiencies noted.	Fasu.

—2—

Army Form C. 2118

WAR DIARY
of A.D.V.S., 19th Division.
INTELLIGENCE SUMMARY
(Erase heading not required.)

Instructions regarding War Diaries and Intelligence Summaries are contained in F. S. Regs., Part II. and the Staff Manual respectively. Title Pages will be prepared in manuscript.

Place	Date 1916.	Hour	Summary of Events and Information	Remarks and references to Appendices
FLESSELLES	JUNE 1.		Arrival of troop of III Corps Cavalry (Duke of Lancaster's Own Yeomanry.) Visited D.V.S., at ABBEVILLE.	
	2.		Weekly conference of Veterinary Officers.	
	3.		Lieut. T. Menzies left on leave. Visited ABBEVILLE AREA.	
	4.		Inspected Signal Coy., D.H.Q., etc.	
	5.		Inspected A/89 and B/89 F.A.Bdes. Visited ABBEVILLE.	
	6.		Routine work. Inspected 21st Mobile Veterinary Section and other Divisional Troops.	
	7.		Section D.A.C. left for forward area. Routine work and inspections.	
	8.		To ABBEVILLE.	
	9.		Weekly conference of Veterinary Officers.	
	10.		Reported that Clerk, No. S/4/090120 Pte. T.E.MORGAN was admitted to Field Ambulance - sick. Inspected 7th East Lancs. Regiment.	
	11.		Visited ABBEVILLE.	
	12.		Inspected East Lancs. Regt. and 19th Divl. Signal Company.	
	13.		Inspected remounts at LONGPRE.	
	14.		Inspected 7th Bn. King's Own Royal Lancaster Regiment.	
	15.		Pte. Morgan, A.S.C., (clerk) evacuated. Weekly conference of Vety. Officers. 29 animals evacuated.	
ST GRATIEN	16.		Moved to ST. GRATIEN. Office at Mairie. 31st M.V.S. to FRECHENCOURT. Inspected various units.	

Army Form C. 2118

WAR DIARY
or
INTELLIGENCE SUMMARY, 19th Division.
(Erase heading not required.)

Instructions regarding War Diaries and Intelligence Summaries are contained in F. S. Regs., Part II. and the Staff Manual respectively. Title Pages will be prepared in manuscript.

Place	Date	Hour	Summary of Events and Information	Remarks and references to Appendices
ST GRATIEN	1916. JUNE. 17.		No. S/4/093594, Private L. ALLINGHAM, A.S.C., reported as clerk. Inspected No. 155 Coy. A.S.C., Signal Coy., and M.M.P.	
	18.		Conference at Office of D.D.V.S., Fourth Army.	
	19.		a/S.Sergt. J. LOW, No. 147, A.V.C., despatched to No. 7 Veterinary Hospital, FORGES-LES-EAUX. Routine work and inspections.	
	20.		Advanced collecting station established at LAVIEVILLE. Evacuated 10 animals.	
	21.		Inspected 9/Royal Welsh Fusiliers, 9th Cheshires and Signal Company.	
	22.		Routine work and inspected 31st Mobile Veterinary Section.	
	23.		Inspected 53rd Reserve Park, A.S.C.	
	24.		Evacuated 15 horses. Inspected 19th Divl. Ammunition Column.	
	25.		Routine work and inspections of local units.	
	26.		Routine work. Inspections.	
	27.		Evacuated 45 horses. Inspected 19th Signal Coy.	
	28.		Inspections of various units. Routine work.	
	29.		Inspected 31st M.V.S., D.H.Q., etc.	
	30.		Left ST. GRATIEN. Arrived MILLENCOURT.	
			Weather generally fine, but heavy rain during last few days of month.	

F.A.S Lloyd Major
A.D.V.S.
19 Division

WAR DIARY
INTELLIGENCE SUMMARY

of A.D.V.S., 19th Division.

(Erase heading not required.)

Army Form C. 2118

Instructions regarding War Diaries and Intelligence Summaries are contained in F. S. Regs., Part II. and the Staff Manual respectively. Title Pages will be prepared in manuscript.

Place	Date 1916.	Hour	Summary of Events and Information	Remarks and references to Appendices
FLESSELLES	JUNE 1.		Arrival of troop of III Corps Cavalry (Duke of Lancaster's Own Yeomanry.) Visited D.V.S., at ABBEVILLE.	A.S.U.
	2.		Weekly conference of Veterinary Officers.	A.S.U.
	3.		Lieut. T. Menzies left on leave. Visited ABBEVILLE AREA.	A.S.U.
	4.		Inspected Signal Coy., D.H.Q., etc.	A.S.U.
	5.		Inspected A/89 and B/89 F.A.Bdes. Visited ABBEVILLE.	A.S.U.
	6.		Routine work. Inspected 21st Mobile Veterinary Section and other Divisional Troops.	A.S.U.
	7.		Section D.A.C. left for forward area. Routine work and inspections.	A.S.U.
	8.		To ABBEVILLE.	A.S.U.
	9.		Weekly conference of Veterinary Officers.	A.S.U.
	10.		Reported that Clerk, No. S/4/090120 Pte. T.E.MORGAN was admitted to Field Ambulance - sick. Inspected 7th East Lancs. Regiment.	A.S.U.
	11.		Visited ABBEVILLE.	A.S.U.
	12.		Inspected East Lancs. Regt. and 19th Divl. Signal Company.	A.S.U.
	13.		Inspected remounts at LONGPRE.	A.S.U.
	14.		Inspected 7th Bn. King's Own Royal Lancaster Regiment.	A.S.U.
	15.		Pte. Morgan, A.S.C., (clerk) evacuated. Weekly conference of Vety. Officers. 29 animals evacuated.	A.S.U.
ST GRATIEN	16.		Moved to ST. GRATIEN. Office at Mairie. 31st M.V.S. to FRECHENCOURT. Inspected various units.	A.S.U.

Army Form C. 2118

WAR DIARY

of A.D.V.S., 19th Division.

INTELLIGENCE SUMMARY

(Erase heading not required.)

Instructions regarding War Diaries and Intelligence Summaries are contained in F.S. Regs., Part II. and the Staff Manual respectively. Title Pages will be prepared in manuscript.

Place	Date 1916.	Hour	Summary of Events and Information	Remarks and references to Appendices
ST. GRATIEN	JUNE. 17.		No. S/4/093594, Private L. ALLINGHAM, A.S.C., reported as clerk. Inspected No. 155 Coy. A.S.C., Signal Coy., and M.M.P.	F.a.s.u.
	18.		Conference at Office of D.D.V.S., Fourth Army.	F.a.s.u.
	19.		a/S.Sergt. J. LOW, No. 147, A.V.C., despatched to No. 7 Veterinary Hospital, FORGES-LES-EAUX. Routine work and inspections.	F.a.s.u.
	20.		Advanced collecting station established at LAVIEVILLE. Evacuated 10 animals.	F.a.s.u.
	21.		Inspected 8/Royal Welsh Fusiliers, 9th Cheshires and Signal Company.	F.a.s.u.
	22.		Routine work and inspected 31st Mobile Veterinary Section.	F.a.s.u.
	23.		Inspected 33rd Reserve Park, A.S.C.	F.a.s.u.
	24.		Evacuated 13 horses. Inspected 19th Divl. Ammunition Column.	F.a.s.u.
	25.		Routine work and inspections of local units.	F.a.s.u.
	26.		Routine work. Inspections.	F.a.s.u.
	27.		Evacuated 43 horses. Inspected 19th Signal Coy.	F.a.s.u.
	28.		Inspections of various units. Routine work.	F.a.s.u.
	29.		Inspected 31st M.V.S., D.H.Q., etc.	F.a.s.u.
	30.		Left ST. GRATIEN. Arrived MILLENCOURT. Weather generally fine, but heavy rain during last few days of month.	F.a.s.u.

F.a.g.Lloore Major A.v.c.
A.D.V.S.
19 June 1916

Army Form C. 2118

Vol 11

WAR DIARY

INTELLIGENCE SUMMARY

of A.D.V.S., 19th Division.

(Erase heading not required.)

Instructions regarding War Diaries and Intelligence Summaries are contained in F. S. Regs., Part II. and the Staff Manual respectively. Title Pages will be prepared in manuscript.

Place	Date 1916.	Hour	Summary of Events and Information	Remarks and references to Appendices
MILLENCOURT	July 1.		Inspected local units. Established advanced collecting station at ALBERT on ALBERT-AMIENS Road.	
	2.		Inspections and routine work.	
	3.		Selected Collecting Post at ALBERT.	
	4.		Inspected D.H.Q. and local units.	
	5.		Routine work and inspections.	
	6.		Routine work and inspections of Infantry Brigades.	
	7.		Weekly conference of Veterinary Officers at Office. Inspected 19th Divl. Signal Coy.	
	8.		Routine work and inspected R.E.	
	9.		Inspections of various small units.	
	10.		Inspected 59th Field Ambulance.	
	11.		Inspected 81st, 82nd and 94th Field Companies, R.E., 5th South Wales Borderers (Pioneers) and 9th Royal Welsh Fusiliers.	
	12.		D.H.Q. moved to HENENCOURT. Office at RUE de BAS.	
HENENCOURT	13.		Inspection of all Farriers' wallets, deficiencies and condition noted.	
	14.		Weekly conference of Veterinary Officers at Office.	
	15.		Inspections and routine.	
	16.		Inspected Signal Coy. and M.M.P. horses.	

-1-

Army Form C. 2118

WAR DIARY
or
INTELLIGENCE SUMMARY

of A.D.V.S., 19th Division.

(Erase heading not required.)

Instructions regarding War Diaries and Intelligence Summaries are contained in F. S. Regs., Part II. and the Staff Manual respectively. Title Pages will be prepared in manuscript.

Place	Date 1916.	Hour	Summary of Events and Information	Remarks and references to Appendices
HENENCOURT.	July. 17.		Inspected D.H.Q. and Infantry transport.	
	18.		Routine work.	
	19.		To MERICOURT to inspect remounts arriving.	
	20.		Moved to ALBERT. Office at RUE de BRAY.	
ALBERT.	21.		Weekly conference of Veterinary Officers at Office.	
	22.		M.V.S. moved to ALBERT. Inspected D.A.C. and selected 30 animals for evacuation for debility.	
	24.		O.C. Mobile Veterinary Section took over veterinary charge of III Corps H.A. Group. M.V.S. moved to LAVIEVILLE. Advanced collecting post established at E.12.a.6.9.	
	25.		Inspected 86th Brigade and 87th Brigade, R.F.A.	
	26.		Inspected 88th Brigade and 89th Brigade, R.F.A.	
	27.		Lieut. Menzies took over temporary veterinary charge of 2nd Indian F. Squadron, R.E. Inspected 19th Divl. Signal Company.	
	28.		Weekly conference of veterinary officers at office in morning. Afternoon, attended conference at D.D.V.S' Office, Fourth Army.	
	29.		No. 7259, a/Sergt. A.T.VAUGHAN, A.V.C., A/89th Brigade, R.F.A. killed by shell fire. Inspected D.A.C.	
	30.		Moved to BAIZIEUX. Office at Chateau.	

Jas Moore Major
A.D.V.S. 19th Division

-2-

Army Form C. 2118

WAR DIARY
or
INTELLIGENCE SUMMARY 19th Division.
(Erase heading not required.)

Instructions regarding War Diaries and Intelligence Summaries are contained in F.S. Regs., Part II. and the Staff Manual respectively. Title Pages will be prepared in manuscript.

Place	Date	Hour	Summary of Events and Information	Remarks and references to Appendices
MILLENCOURT.	1916. July 1.		Inspected local units. Established advanced collecting station at ALBERT on ALBERT-AMIENS Road.	
	2.		Inspections and routine work.	
	3.		Selected Collecting Post at ALBERT.	
	4.		Inspected D.H.Q. and local units.	
	5.		Routine work and inspections.	
	6.		Routine work and inspections of Infantry Brigades.	
	7.		Weekly conference of Veterinary Officers at Office. Inspected 19th Divl. Signal Coy.	
	8.		Routine work and inspected R.A.	
	9.		Inspections of various small units.	
	10.		Inspected 59th Field Ambulance.	
	11.		Inspected 81st, 82nd and 94th Field Companies, R.E., 5th South Wales Borderers (Pioneers) and 9th Royal Welsh Fusiliers.	
	12.		D.H.Q. moved to HENENCOURT. Office at RUE de BAS.	
HENENCOURT.	13.		Inspection of all Farriers' wallets, deficiencies and condition noted.	
	14.		Weekly conference of Veterinary Officers at Office.	
	15.		Inspections and routine.	
	16.		Inspected Signal Coy. and M.M.P. horses.	

-1-

WAR DIARY
or
INTELLIGENCE SUMMARY of A.D.V.S. 19th Division.

(Erase heading not required.)

Army Form C. 2118

Place	Date	Hour	Summary of Events and Information	Remarks and references to Appendices
HENENCOURT.	1916. July. 17.		Inspected D.H.Q. and Infantry transport.	
	18.		Routine work.	
	19.		To MERICOURT to inspect remounts arriving.	
	20.		Moved to ALBERT. Office at RUE de BRAY.	
ALBERT.	21.		Weekly conference of Veterinary Officers at Office.	
	22.		M.V.S. moved to ALBERT. Inspected D.A.C. and selected 30 animals for evacuation for debility.	
	24.		O.C. Mobile Veterinary Section took over veterinary charge of III Corps H.A. Group. M.V.S. moved to LAVIEVILLE. Advanced collecting post established at E.12.a.6.9.	
	25.		Inspected 56th Brigade and 57th Brigade, R.F.A.	
	26.		Inspected 88th Brigade and 89th Brigade, R.F.A.	
	27.		Lieut. Menzies took over temporary veterinary charge of 2nd Indian F. Squadron, R.E. Inspected 19th Divl. Signal Company.	
	28.		Weekly conference of veterinary officers at office in morning. Afternoon, attended conference at D.D.V.S.' Office, Fourth Army.	
	29.		No. 7259, a/Sergt. A.T.VAUGHAN, A.V.C., A/89th Brigade, R.F.A. killed by shell fire. Inspected D.A.C.	
	31.		Moved to BAIZIEUX. Office at Chateau.	

-2-

J.a.S.Moore Major
N.C.
A.D.V.S 14 Division
19

Army Form C. 2118

Vol 12

WAR DIARY

of A.D.V.S.,

INTELLIGENCE SUMMARY. 19th Division.

(Erase heading not required.)

Instructions regarding War Diaries and Intelligence Summaries are contained in F.S. Regs., Part II. and the Staff Manual respectively. Title Pages will be prepared in manuscript.

Place	Date 1916.	Hour	Summary of Events and Information	Remarks and references to Appendices
BAIZIEUX.	August 1.		Routine Work.	
	2.		Evacuated 24 animals to Base.	
	3.		Moved to LONG.	
LONG.	4.		Transferred No. 1567, U/A/Sgt. BULLOCK (reverted from P.a/Sgt.) to No. 2 Hospital, HAVRE.	
	5.		Inspected local Units.	
	6.		Left for BAILLEUL. M.V.S. evacuated 3 horses.	
ST.Jans CAPPEL.	7.		Arrived at ST. JANS CAPPEL. Called on A.D.V.S., 50th Division, at WESTOUTRE.	
WESTOUTRE.	8.		Arrived at WESTOUTRE.	
	9.		Inspected 56 Coy. M.G.Corps and 57 Coy. M.G.Corps.	
	10.		Inspected 250th Tunnelling Coy. and A/88th Bde. R.F.A.	
	11.		Conference of Veterinary Officers at Office. Conducting party with 9 horses left for Base.	
	12.		Attended conference of A.DsV.S. at BAILLEUL.	
	13.		Inspected D.H.Q., Signals and M.V.S.	
	14.		Evacuated 15 animals. Inspected D.A.C.	
	15.		Inspected 89th Brigade, R.F.A.	
	16.		Inspected 86th Brigade, R.F.A.	
	17.		Inspected 88th Brigade, R.F.A.,	

Army Form C. 2118

WAR DIARY
of A.D.V.S.,
INTELLIGENCE SUMMARY 19th Division.

(Erase heading not required.)

Instructions regarding War Diaries and Intelligence Summaries are contained in F.S. Regs., Part II. and the Staff Manual respectively. Title Pages will be prepared in manuscript.

Place	Date 1916	Hour	Summary of Events and Information	Remarks and references to Appendices
WESTOUTRE	August 18.		Conference of Veterinary Officers at Office. Inspected Signal Company.	
	19.		Captain J.H. SHERLOCK, A.V.C., (88th and 89th Brigades, R.F.A.,) sick in hospital.	
	20.		M.V.S. evacuated 22 animals by special train.	
	21.		Inspections and routine.	
	22.		Inspected M.V.S. and 19th Signal Company.	
	23.		Routine work.	
	24.		Inspected 56th Infantry Brigade.	
	25.		Conference of Veterinary Officers at Office.	
	26.		No. 465, a/Sgt. P. Woodger, of M.V.S., admitted to Field Ambulance for injury to foot. Inspected D.H.Q.	
	27.		Inspected IX Corps Cavalry. Inspected dog for rabies at LA CLYTTE.	
	28.		21 horses and 3 mules left by road for ST. OMER to Receiving Hospital. Inspected Nos. 2 and 4 Sections, D.A.C.	
	29.		Inspected D/89th Brigade. D.D.V.S. called.	
	30.		Notified of evacuation of Sgt. Woodger, M.V.S.	
	31.		Inspected local units. Routine work. **************** Weather - Early part of month, fine. Letter part of month, very wet and colder.	

-2-

Army Form C. 2118

WAR DIARY
of
INTELLIGENCE SUMMARY. 19th Division.
(Erase heading not required.)

Instructions regarding War Diaries and Intelligence Summaries are contained in F. S. Regs., Part II. and the Staff Manual respectively. Title Pages will be prepared in manuscript.

Place	Date 1916.	Hour	Summary of Events and Information	Remarks and references to Appendices
BAIZIEUX.	August 1.		Routine Work.	
	2.		Evacuated 24 animals to Base.	
	3.		Moved to LONG.	
LONG.	4.		Transferred No. 1567, U/A/Sgt. BULLOCK (reverted from P.s/Sgt.) to No. 2 Hospital, HAVRE.	
	5.		Inspected local Units.	
	6.		Left for BAILLEUL. M.V.S. evacuated 3 horses.	
ST.Jans CAPPEL.	7.		Arrived at ST. JANS CAPPEL. Called on A.D.V.S., 50th Division, at WESTOUTRE.	
WESTOUTRE.	8.		Arrived at WESTOUTRE.	
	9.		Inspected 56 Coy. M.G.Corps and 57 Coy. M.G.Corps.	
	10.		Inspected 250th Tunnelling Coy. and A/88th Bde. R.F.A.	
	11.		Conference of Veterinary Officers at Office. Conducting party with 9 horses left for Base.	
	12.		Attended conference of A.D.V.S. at BAILLEUL.	
	13.		Inspected D.H.Q., Signals and M.V.S.	
	14.		Evacuated 15 animals. Inspected D.A.C.	
	15.		Inspected 89th Brigade, R.F.A.	
	16.		Inspected 86th Brigade, R.F.A.	
	17.		Inspected 88th Brigade, R.F.A.	

Army Form C. 2118

WAR DIARY
INTELLIGENCE SUMMARY of A.D.V.S. 19th Division.
(Erase heading not required.)

Instructions regarding War Diaries and Intelligence Summaries are contained in F.S. Regs., Part II. and the Staff Manual respectively. Title Pages will be prepared in manuscript.

Place	Date 1916 August	Hour	Summary of Events and Information	Remarks and references to Appendices
WESTOUTRE	18.		Conference of Veterinary Officers at Office. Inspected Signal Company.	
	19.		Captain J.H. SHERLOCK, A.V.C., (88th and 89th Brigades, R.F.A.,) sick in hospital.	
	20.		M.V.S. evacuated 22 animals by special train.	
	21.		Inspections and routine.	
	22.		Inspected M.V.S. and 19th Signal Company.	
	23.		Routine work.	
	24.		Inspected 56th Infantry Brigade.	
	25.		Conference of Veterinary Officers at Office.	
	26.		No. 465, a/Sgt. P. Woodger, of M.V.S., admitted to Field Ambulance for injury to foot. Inspected D.H.Q.	
	27.		Inspected IX Corps Cavalry. Inspected dog for rabies at LA CLYTTE.	
	28.		21 horses and 3 miles left by road for ST. OMER to Receiving Hospital. Inspected Nos. 2 and 4 Sections, D.A.C.	
	29.		Inspected D/89th Brigade. D.D.V.S. called.	
	30.		Notified of evacuation of Sgt. Woodger, M.V.S.	
	31.		Inspected local units. Routine work.	
			*************************	
			Weather – Early part of month, fine. Latter part of month, very wet and colder.	

-2-

Army Form C. 2118

Vol/3

WAR DIARY of A.D.V.S., 19th Division.

~~INTELLIGENCE SUMMARY~~

(Erase heading not required.)

Instructions regarding War Diaries and Intelligence Summaries are contained in F.S. Regs., Part II. and the Staff Manual respectively. Title Pages will be prepared in manuscript.

Place	Date 1916	Hour	Summary of Events and Information	Remarks and references to Appendices
WESTOUTRE.	Septr. 1.		Conference of Veterinary Officers at Office. Routine work.	
	2.		Inspected 5th South Wales Borderers, 9th Entrenching Battalion, 59th Field Ambulance, 58th Coy. Machine Gun Corps, 56 Coy., Machine Gun Corps.	
	3.		Inspected Corps Troops.	
	4.		To BAILLEUL to see A.D.V.S., 12th Division. Evacuated 42 Animals.	
	5.		Inspected H.Q. Coy., 19th Divisional Train.	
	6.		Moved to BAILLEUL – Office Rue de Lille. 31st Mobile Veterinary Section moved to ~~NIEPPE~~ NIEPPE. M.V.S. transferred to O.C., 4th Canadian M.V.S. 33 sick horses.	
BAILLEUL.	7.		Inspected No. 3 Coy., Divisional Train.	
	8.		Conference of Veterinary Officers.	
	9.		Inspected 81st, 82nd and 94th Field Coys., R.E.	
	10.		Inspected D.H.Q. and Signal Coy.	
	11.		Inspected animals of 89th Brigade, R.F.A. prior to reorganisation of Divisional Artillery.	
	12.		Inspected No. 4 Sec. D.A.C.	
	13.		Inspections of Infantry Units.	
	14.		3 Sergeants, A.V.C., surplus through reorganisation of Divisional Artillery, despatched to No. 2 Veterinary Hospital, HAVRE. Inspected No. 4 Sec. D.A.C. Evacuated 5 animals.	
	15.		Weekly conference of Veterinary Officers. Evacuated 45 animals by road to ST. OMER.	
	16.		Inspected 31st Mobile Veterinary Section. D.D.V.S. called.	

1875 Wt. W593/826 1,000,000 4/15 J.B.C. & A. A.D.S.S./Forms/C.2118. —1—

Army Form C. 2118

WAR DIARY of A.D.V.S., 19th Division.

INTELLIGENCE SUMMARY

(Erase heading not required.)

Instructions regarding War Diaries and Intelligence Summaries are contained in F.S. Regs., Part II. and the Staff Manual respectively. Title Pages will be prepared in manuscript.

Place	Date Septr.	Hour	Summary of Events and Information	Remarks and references to Appendices
BAILLEUL	17.		Routine and inspection of D.H.Q. and M.M.P. Evacuated 15 animals.	
	18.		Inspection of Divl. Signal Company.	
	19.		Routine work and inspections. Evacuated 16 animals by barge. Evacuated 10 animals.	
	20.		Moved to MERRIS.	
MERRIS.	21.		Inspection of M.V.S. Evacuated 13 animals by barge.	
	22.		Weekly conference of Veterinary Officers. Inspected Signal Company and M.M.P.	
	23.		Inspected 57th Field Ambulance and 57th Infantry Brigade.	
	24.		Inspected 31st Mobile Veterinary Section. Evacuated 10 animals by barge from ESTAIRES.	
	25.		Routine work and inspection of local units. D.D.V.S. called.	
	26.		To. Mobile Veterinary Section. Evacuated 11 animals by barge.	
	27.		D.D.V.S. called and inspected 88th Brigade, R.F.A.	
	28.		Inspected 56th Infy. Bde. Evacuated 13 animals.	
	29.		Weekly conference of Veterinary Officers at Office.	
	30.		Attended conference at BAILLEUL.	

****

-2-

Army Form C. 2118

WAR DIARY

of A.D.V.S.,

INTELLIGENCE SUMMARY 19th Division.

(Erase heading not required.)

Instructions regarding War Diaries and Intelligence Summaries are contained in F.S. Regs., Part II. and the Staff Manual respectively. Title Pages will be prepared in manuscript.

Place	Date 1916	Hour	Summary of Events and Information	Remarks and references to Appendices
WESTOUTRE.	Septr. 1.		Conference of Veterinary Officers at Office. Routine work.	
	2.		Inspected 5th South Wales Borderers, 9th Entrenching Battalion, 59th Field Ambulance, 58th Coy. Machine Gun Corps, 56 Coy., Machine Gun Corps.	
	3.		Inspected Corps Troops.	
	4.		To BAILLEUL to see A.D.V.S., 12th Division. Evacuated 42 Animals.	
	5.		Inspected H.Q. Coy., 19th Divisional Train.	
	6.		Moved to BAILLEUL - Office Rue de Lille. 31st Mobile Veterinary Section moved to NIEPPE. M.V.S. transferred to O.C. 4th Canadian M.V.S. 33 sick horses.	
BAILLEUL.	7.		Inspected No. 3 Coy., Divisional Train.	
	8.		Conference of Veterinary Officers.	
	9.		Inspected 81st, 82nd and 94th Field Coys., R.E.	
	10.		Inspected D.H.Q. and Signal Coy.	
	11.		Inspected animals of 89th Brigade, R.F.A. prior to reorganisation of Divisional Artillery.	
	12.		Inspected No. 4 Sec. D.A.C.	
	13.		Inspections of Infantry Units.	
	14.		3 Sergeants, A.V.C., surplus through reorganisation of Divisional Artillery, despatched to No. 2 Veterinary Hospital, HAVRE. Inspected No. 4 Sec. D.A.C. Evacuated 5 animals.	
	15.		Weekly conference of Veterinary Officers. Evacuated 45 animals by road to ST. OMER.	
	16.		Inspected 31st Mobile Veterinary Section. D.D.V.S. called.	

-1-

WAR DIARY
INTELLIGENCE SUMMARY

Army Form C. 2118

WAR DIARY

INTELLIGENCE SUMMARY of A.D.V.S., 19th Division.

(Erase heading not required.)

Instructions regarding War Diaries and Intelligence Summaries are contained in F. S. Regs, Part II. and the Staff Manual respectively. Title Pages will be prepared in manuscript.

Place	Date 1916.	Hour	Summary of Events and Information	Remarks and references to Appendices
MERRIS.	Nov. 1.		Inspected 8th (S) Bn. Gloucestershire Regiment.	
	2.		M.V.S. moved to farm near MERRIS. Inspected Signal Company and D.H.Q.	
	3.		Inspected various Infantry units.	
	4.		Inspections and routine work.	
	5.		Left for MARIEUX via DOULLENS by train.	
MARIEUX.	6.		M.V.S. arrived and occupied billets near AUTHIE. D.D.V.S. called.	
	7.		D.H.Q. moved to AUTHIE. Inspected Signal Company and 10th (S) Bn. Worcestershire Regiment.	
AUTHIE.	8.		M.V.S. moved to AUTHIE. 165 and 170 Brigades, R.F.A. attached. Inspected M.V.S.	
	9.		A/87, D/86, D/87 Brigades, R.F.A. inspected. Attended conference of D.D.V.S.	
	10.		Inspected 10th Worcester, 8th North Stafford and 8th Gloucester Regiments.	
	11.		Inspection of wallets. Inspected D/87, A/87, A/86 Brigades, R.F.A.	
	12.		Inspected D.A.C.	
	13.		Weekly conference of Veterinary Officers at Office.	
	14.		Inspected C/88, D/88 Brigades, R.F.A.	
	15.		Inspected Signal Company, D.H.Q., and other local units.	
	16.		Inspected 81st, 82nd and 94th Field Companies, R.E.	
	17.		Office moved with D.H.Q. to RUBEMPRE. M.V.S. to CONTAY.	

-1-

WAR DIARY

INTELLIGENCE SUMMARY of A.D.V.S., 19th Division.

October 1916

Vol 14

Army Form C. 2118

(Erase heading not required.)

Place	Date 1916.	Hour	Summary of Events and Information	Remarks and references to Appendices
MERRIS.	Oct. 1.		Inspected 8th (S) Bn. Gloucestershire Regiment.	
	2.		M.V.S. moved to farm near MERRIS. Inspected Signal Company and D.H.Q.	
	3.		Inspected various Infantry units.	
	4.		Inspections and routine work.	
	5.		Left for MARIEUX via DOULLENS by train.	
MARIEUX.	6.		M.V.S. arrived and occupied billets near AUTHIE. D.D.V.S. called.	
	7.		D.H.Q. moved to AUTHIE. Inspected Signal Company and 10th (S) Bn. Worcestershire Regiment.	
AUTHIE.	8.		M.V.S. moved to AUTHIE. 165 and 170 Brigades, R.F.A. attached. Inspected M.V.S.	
	9.		A/87, D/86, D/87 Brigades, R.F.A. inspected. Attended conference of D.D.V.S.	
	10.		Inspected 10th Worcester, 8th North Stafford and 8th Gloucester Regiments.	
	11.		Inspection of wallets. Inspected D/87, A/87, A/86 Brigades, R.F.A.	
	12.		Inspected D.A.C.	
	13.		Weekly conference of Veterinary Officers at Office.	
	14.		Inspected C/88, D/88 Brigades, R.F.A.	
	15.		Inspected Signal Company, D.H.Q., and other local units.	
	16.		Inspected 81st, 82nd and 94th Field Companies, R.E.	
	18.		Office moved with D.H.Q. to RUBEMPRE. M.V.S. to CONTAY.	

-1-

Army Form C. 2118

WAR DIARY of A.D.V.S., 19th Division.

INTELLIGENCE SUMMARY

(Erase heading not required.)

Instructions regarding War Diaries and Intelligence Summaries are contained in F.S. Regs., Part II. and the Staff Manual respectively. Title Pages will be prepared in manuscript.

Place	Date 1916.	Hour	Summary of Events and Information	Remarks and references to Appendices
RUBEMPRE.	Novr. 18.		Local units inspected.	
	19.		Inspections and routine work.	
	20.		Conference of Veterinary Officers at Office. Inspected 9th Welsh, 6th Wilts, and 9th Cheshire Regiments and 58 Coy., Machine Gun Corps.	
	21.		D.H.Q. moved to WARLOY. M.V.S. to BOUZINCOURT.	
WARLOY.	22.		Inspections and routine work.	
	23.		D.H.Q. moved to BOUZINCOURT CAMP. Artillery of 11th, 17th and 2 5th Divisions attached.	
BOUZINCOURT	24.		Inspections and routine work.	
	25.		Inspected 82nd and 94th Field Coys. R.E.	
	26.		Inspections of M.V.S. and Signal Company.	
	27.		Veterinary Officers of 19th Division and 11th and 25th Divisional Artillery at Office.	
	28.		D.D.V.S. called. Veterinary Officers of 17th Divisional Artillery at Office.	
	29.		Advanced Collecting Post established at CRUCIFIX CORNER.	
	30.		Captain H. BONE, A.V.C., O.C. 31st Mobile Veterinary Section left to take over duties of A.D.V.S., 8th Division.	
	31.		Inspections and routine work.	

****

Weather has been exceedingly wet during the latter part of the month.

—2—

Army Form C. 2118

WAR DIARY of A.D.V.S.,
INTELLIGENCE SUMMARY 19th Division.
(Erase heading not required.)

Instructions regarding War Diaries and Intelligence Summaries are contained in F.S. Regs., Part II. and the Staff Manual respectively. Title Pages will be prepared in manuscript.

Place	Date 1916.	Hour	Summary of Events and Information	Remarks and references to Appendices
RUBEMPRE.	~~Nov~~ Oct. 18.		Local units inspected.	
	19.		Inspections and routine work.	
	20.		Conference of Veterinary Officers at Office. Inspected 9th Welsh, 8th Wilts, and 9th Cheshire Regiments and 58 Coy., Machine Gun Corps.	
WARLOY.	21.		D.H.Q. moved to WARLOY. M.V.S. to BOUZINCOURT.	
	22.		Inspections and routine work.	
	23.		D.H.Q. moved to BOUZINCOURT CAMP. Artillery of 11th, 17th and 25th Divisions attached.	
BOUZINCOURT	24.		Inspections and routine work.	
	25.		Inspected 82nd and 94th Field Coys. R.E.	
	26.		Inspections of M.V.S. and Signal Company.	
	27.		Veterinary Officers of 19th Division and 11th and 25th Divisional Artillery at Office.	
	28.		D.D.V.S. called. Veterinary Officers of 17th Divisional Artillery at Office.	
	29.		Advanced Collecting Post established at CRUCIFIX CORNER.	
	30.		Captain H. BONE, A.V.C., O.C. 31st Mobile Veterinary Section left to take over duties of A.D.V.S., 8th Division.	
	31.		Inspections and routine work.	
			************	
			Weather has been exceedingly wet during the latter part of the month.	

Jas Moore Major C.
A.D.V.S.
19 Division

-2-

WAR DIARY

INTELLIGENCE SUMMARY

of A.D.V.S., 19th Division.

(Erase heading not required.)

Army Form C. 2118

Instructions regarding War Diaries and Intelligence Summaries are contained in F.S. Regs., Part II. and the Staff Manual respectively. Title Pages will be prepared in manuscript.

Place	Date 1916.	Hour	Summary of Events and Information	Remarks and references to Appendices
BOUZINCOURT	Nov. 1.		Inspected 58th and 59th Brigades, R.F.A. (11th Division). M.V.S. evacuated 62 animals.	
	2.		D.D.V.S. called and inspected animals of 17th Division at M.V.S. prior to evacuation.	
	3.		Inspected 111th Brigade, R.F.A. (25th Division), 133rd Brigade R.F.A. (11th Division). Weekly conference of Veterinary Officers at Office. Lieut. H.W.STEVENS, A.V.C., reported for duty and took over veterinary charge of Infantry Brigades of Division. 58 animals evacuated. To. 11th Division R.A. H.Q.	
	4.		A.D.V.S., 11th Division and self inspected 58th, 59th and 60th Bdes. R.F.A. (11th Division). 22 animals evacuated.	
	5.		Inspected 34th Coy., Machine Gun Corps, 58th Field Ambulance, 88th and 87th Bdes., R.F.A.	
	6.		Inspected M.V.S., D.H.Q. and Signal Company. 58 animals evacuated.	
	7.		Inspected 59th (11th Division), 112th and 113th Bdes., R.F.A. (25th Division) with D.D.V.S. 32 animals evacuated.	
	8.		40 animals evacuated. Animal strength of Division and attached units - 13492.	
	9.		Weekly conference at Office. D.D.V.S. called. 32 animals evacuated.	
	10.		Inspected D.A.C. and 88th Brigade, R.F.A. 42 animals evacuated.	
	11.		Inspected 11th D.A.C. 40 animals evacuated by M.V.S.	
	12.		Inspected 78th Bde., R.F.A. (17th Division) and 11th D.A.C. 40 animals evacuated.	
	13.		Inspected 25th D.A.C. and 25th Divisional Train.	

-1-

WAR DIARY

INTELLIGENCE SUMMARY

of A.D.V.S., 19th Division.

(Erase heading not required.)

Army Form C.2118

Place	Date 1916.	Hour	Summary of Events and Information	Remarks and references to Appendices
BOUZINCOURT.	Novr. 15.		Inspected 79th Brigade R.F.A. (17th Division.) 48 animals evacuated.	
	16.		Inspected 87th Brigade, R.F.A., 81st Brigade R.F.A. and Section Signal Company attached 58th Infantry Brigade, 9th Welsh Regiment and 9th Cheshire Regiment. 32 animals evacuated.	
	17.		Veterinary Officers report at Office. Inspected 113th Brigade R.F.A. (25th Division).	
	18.		Inspected 19th Divl. Signal Company. 34 animals evacuated.	
	19.		Inspected D.H.Q. and M.V.S. 50 animals evacuated.	
	20.		D.D.V.S. called and inspected 113th Brigade R.F.A. (25th Division.) Forwarded record of MALLEIN test of animals of 515 Howitzer Battery (C/85th Brigade, R.F.A.) No reactions.	
	21.		Inspected Secs. 3 and 4, 19th Divl. Signal Coy. 36 animals evacuated.	
	22.		Inspected D/88th Brigade R.F.A. and D/60 Brigade, R.F.A. (11th Division). Advanced Collecting Post at CRUCIFIX CORNER recalled. 48 animals evacuated. 22 turned over to 22nd V.V.S. (11th Division).	
CONTAY.	23.		Moved to CONTAY.	
DOULLENS.	24.		Moved to DOULLENS.	
BERNAVILLE.	25.		Moved to BERNAVILLE.	
	26.		Inspected M.V.S.	
	27.		Routine work.	
	28.		Inspected No. 1 Coy., A.S.C., 19th Divisional Train at MARTINSART. Called on Town Major, AUTHIEULE re 7 horses left with him for debility.	

-2-

WAR DIARY of A.D.V.S., 19th Division.

INTELLIGENCE SUMMARY

(Erase heading not required.)

Army Form C. 2118

Instructions regarding War Diaries and Intelligence Summaries are contained in F.S. Regs., Part II. and the Staff Manual respectively. Title Pages will be prepared in manuscript.

Place	Date 1916.	Hour	Summary of Events and Information	Remarks and references to Appendices
BERNAVILLE	Novr. 29.		Inspections of local Units.	
	30.		Routine work.	
			*****	
			Weather has been almost continual rains and occasional high winds.	

Lieut. Colonel
A.D.V.S. 19 Division

- 3 -

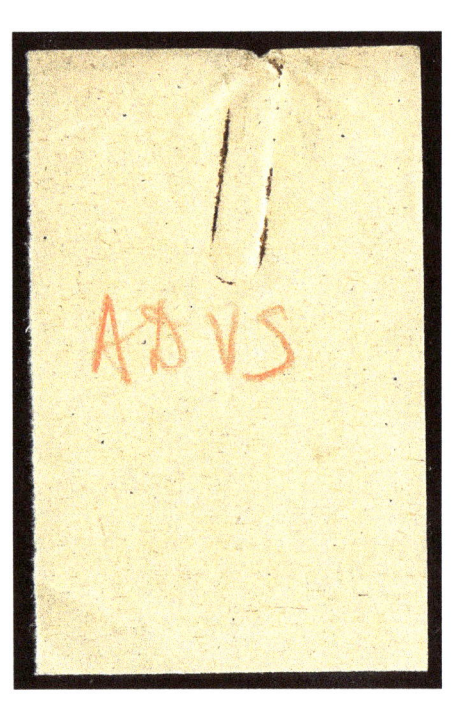

Army Form C.2118

WAR DIARY
or
INTELLIGENCE SUMMARY
A.D.V.S., 19th Division.
(Erase heading not required.)

Instructions regarding War Diaries and Intelligence Summaries are contained in F.S. Regs., Part II. and the Staff Manual respectively. Title Pages will be prepared in manuscript.

Place	Date	Hour	Summary of Events and Information	Remarks and references to Appendices
BOUZINCOURT	1916. Novr. 1.		Inspected 88th and 89th Brigades, R.F.A. (11th Division). M.V.S. evacuated 62 animals.	
	2.		D.D.V.S. called and inspected animals of 11th Division at M.V.S. prior to evacuation.	
	3.		Inspected 111th Brigade, R.F.A. (25th Division), 133rd Brigade R.F.A. (11th Division). Weekly conference of Veterinary Officers at Office. Lieut. H.W.STEVENS, A.V.C., reported for duty and took over veterinary charge of Infantry Brigades of Division. 56 animals evacuated.	
	4.		To 11th Division R.A. H.Q.	
	5.		A.D.V.S., 11th Division and self inspected 58th, 59th and 60th Bdes. R.F.A. (11th Division). 22 animals evacuated.	
	6.		Inspected 34th Coy., Machine Gun Corps, 58th Field Ambulance, 86th and 87th Bdes., R.F.A.	
	7.		Inspected M.V.S., D.H.Q. and Signal Company. 56 animals evacuated.	
	8.		Inspected 59th (11th Division), 112th and 113th Bdes., R.F.A. (25th Division) with D.D.V.S. 32 animals evacuated.	
	9.		40 animals evacuated. Animal strength of Division and attached units - 13492.	
	10.		Weekly conference at Office. D.D.V.S. called. 32 animals evacuated.	
	11.		Inspected D.A.C. and 88th Brigade, R.F.A. 42 animals evacuated.	
	12.		Inspected 11th D.A.C. 40 animals evacuated by M.V.S.	
	13.		Inspected 78th Bde., R.F.A. (17th Division) and 11th D.A.C. 40 animals evacuated.	
	14.		Inspected 25th D.A.C. and 25th Divisional Train.	

Army Form C. 2118

WAR DIARY
INTELLIGENCE SUMMARY of A.D.V.S. 19th Division.

(Erase heading not required.)

Instructions regarding War Diaries and Intelligence Summaries are contained in F.S. Regs., Part II. and the Staff Manual respectively. Title Pages will be prepared in manuscript.

Place	Date 1916	Hour	Summary of Events and Information	Remarks and references to Appendices
BOUZINCOURT.	Novr. 15.		Inspected 79th Brigade R.F.A. (17th Division.) 48 animals evacuated.	
	16.		Inspected 87th Brigade, R.F.A., 81st Brigade R.F.A. and Section Signal Company attached 58th Infantry Brigade, 9th Welsh Regiment and 9th Cheshire Regiment. 32 animals evacuated.	
	17.		Veterinary Officers report at Office. Inspected 113th Brigade R.F.A. (25th Division).	
	18.		Inspected 19th Divl. Signal Company. 34 animals evacuated.	
	19.		Inspected D.H.Q. and M.V.S. 50 animals evacuated.	
	20.		D.D.V.S. called and inspected 113th Brigade R.F.A. (25th Division.) Forwarded record of MALLEIN test of animals of 515 Howitzer Battery (C/86th Brigade, R.F.A.) No reactions.	
	21.		Inspected Secs. 3 and 4, 19th Divl. Signal Coy. 96 animals evacuated.	
	22.		Inspected D/88th Brigade R.F.A. and D/60 Brigade, R.F.A. (11th Division). Advanced Collecting Post at CRUCIFIX CORNER recalled. 48 animals evacuated. 22 turned over to 22nd M.V.S. (11th Division).	
CONTAY.	23.		Moved to CONTAY.	
DOULLENS.	24.		Moved to DOULLENS.	
BERNAVILLE	25.		Moved to BERNAVILLE.	
	26.		Inspected M.V.S.	
	27.		Routine work.	
	28.		Inspected No. 1 Coy., A.S.C., 19th Divisional Train at MARTINSART. Called on Town Major, AUTHIEULE re 7 horses left with him for debility.	

Army Form C. 2118

WAR DIARY
of A.D.V.S.,
INTELLIGENCE SUMMARY
19th Division.

(Erase heading not required.)

Instructions regarding War Diaries and Intelligence Summaries are contained in F. S. Regs., Part II. and the Staff Manual respectively. Title Pages will be prepared in manuscript.

Place	Date 1916.	Hour	Summary of Events and Information	Remarks and references to Appendices
BERNAVILLE	Novr. 29.		Inspections of local Units.	
	30.		Routine work.	
			*****	
			Weather has been almost continual rains and occasional high winds.	

Army Form C. 2118

WAR DIARY
of A.D.V.S.
INTELLIGENCE SUMMARY. 19th Division.
(Erase heading not required.)

Instructions regarding War Diaries and Intelligence Summaries are contained in F. S. Regs., Part II. and the Staff Manual respectively. Title Pages will be prepared in manuscript.

Place	Date	Hour	Summary of Events and Information	Remarks and references to Appendices
	1916.			
BERNAVILLE.	DECR. 1.		Left on leave to England.	
	2 to 13.		On leave. Returned from leave.	
	14.		D.D.V.S. called.	
	15.		Inspected 59th Field Ambulance, 9th Bn. Royal Welsh Fusiliers and 7th Bn. East Lancashire Regt. Conference of Veterinary Officers at Office.	
	16.		Inspected local units.	
	17.		Inspected D.H.Q. and Signal Company.	
	18.		Inspected 9th Welsh, 6th Wilts. & 8th Gloucestershire Regiments.	
	19.		Inspected 86th Brigade, R.F.A.	
	20.		Inspected Mobile Veterinary Section.	
	21.		Lecture by A.D.V.S. to Officers at Divisional School.	
	22.		Conference of Veterinary Officers at Office.	
	23.		Lecture to Officers. Inspected 6th Wilts. Regiment.	
	24.		Inspected D.H.Q.	
	26.		Inspected Mobile Veterinary Section.	
	27.		Inspected local units. Lecture to Officers.	

Army Form C. 2118

WAR DIARY

of A.D.V.S., 19th Division.

(Erase heading not required.)

Place	Date	Hour	Summary of Events and Information	Remarks and references to Appendices
BERNAVILLE	Decr. 1916. 28.		Routine work.	
	29.		Attended conference at RANCHEVAL.	
	30.		Local inspections.	
	31.		Inspected D.H.Q. and 31st Mobile Veterinary Section.	
			* * * * * * * * * *	

Instructions regarding War Diaries and Intelligence Summaries are contained in F.S. Regs., Part II. and the Staff Manual respectively. Title Pages will be prepared in manuscript.

Army Form C. 2118

WAR DIARY
of A.D.V.S.,
INTELLIGENCE SUMMARY 19th Division.

(Erase heading not required.)

Instructions regarding War Diaries and Intelligence Summaries are contained in F.S. Regs., Part II. and the Staff Manual respectively. Title Pages will be prepared in manuscript.

Place	Date 1916.	Hour	Summary of Events and Information	Remarks and references to Appendices
BERNAVILLE.	DECR. 1.		Left on leave to England.	
	2 to 13.		On leave. Returned from leave.	
	14.		D.D.V.S. called.	
	15.		Inspected 59th Field Ambulance, 9th Bn. Royal Welsh Fusiliers and 7th Bn. East Lancashire Regt. Conference of Veterinary Officers at Office.	
	16.		Inspected local units.	
	17.		Inspected D.H.Q. and Signal Company.	
	18.		Inspected 9th Welsh, 6th Wilts. & 8th Gloucestershire Regiments.	
	19.		Inspected 86th Brigade, R.F.A.	
	20.		Inspected Mobile Veterinary Section.	
	21.		Lecture by A.D.V.S. to Officers at Divisional School.	
	22.		Conference of Veterinary Officers at Office.	
	23.		Lecture to Officers. Inspected 6th Wilts. Regiment.	
	24.		Inspected D.H.Q.	
	26.		Inspected Mobile Veterinary Section.	
	27.		Inspected local units. Lecture to Officers.	

1875 Wt. W593/826 1,000,000 4/15 J.B.C. & A. A.D.S.S./Forms/C. 2118.

-1-

Army Form C. 2118

WAR DIARY
of A.D.V.S.
INTELLIGENCE SUMMARY 19th Division.

(Erase heading not required.)

Instructions regarding War Diaries and Intelligence Summaries are contained in F. S. Regs., Part II. and the Staff Manual respectively. Title Pages will be prepared in manuscript.

Place	Date 1916.	Hour	Summary of Events and Information	Remarks and references to Appendices
BERNAVILLE	Decr. 28.		Routine work.	
	29.		Attended conference at RANCHEVAL.	
	30.		Local inspections.	
	31.		Inspected D.H.Q. and 31st Mobile Veterinary Section.	
			* * * * * * * * * *	

Lashmore Major
A.D.V.S.
19th Division

Army Form C. 2118

WAR DIARY of A.D.V.S., 19th Division.

INTELLIGENCE SUMMARY

(Erase heading not required.)

Instructions regarding War Diaries and Intelligence Summaries are contained in F.S. Regs., Part II. and the Staff Manual respectively. Title Pages will be prepared in manuscript.

Place	Date 1917.	Hour	Summary of Events and Information	Remarks and references to Appendices
BERNAVILLE	Jany. 1.		Inspected 19th Divisional Ammunition Column.	
	2.		Inspected 31st Mobile Veterinary Section.	
	3.		Inspected several Local Units.	
	4.		Inspected M.M.P. animals.	
	5.		Conference of Veterinary Officers at Office.	
	6.		D.D.V.S. inspected horses shod with sheet iron out of oil tins as preventative against P.U.N.	
	7.		Inspected 31st Mobile Veterinary Section.	
	8.		Inspected D.H.Q. and Signal Company.	
	9.		Moved to MARIEUX. 31st Mobile Vet. Section to AUTHIE.	
MARIEUX.	10.		Inspected local units.	
	11.		D.H.Q. moved to COUIN. Took over veterinary charge of 32nd Divisional Artillery, 7th Pontoon Park, 9th Labour Battalion, 37th Prisoners of War Company, 6th Cavalry Pioneers.	
COUIN.	12.		Conference of Veterinary Officers at office.	
	13.		Inspected 86th and 87th Brigades, R.F.A.	
	14.		Inspected 19th Divl. Signal Coy.	
	15.		Captain J.J.N.BROWN, A.V.C., left on leave. Inspected 7th Bn. Loyal North Lancs. Regt.	
	16.		32nd Divisional Artillery, except 223rd Field Coy., R.E., left area; also 6th Cav. Pioneers.	
	17.		Inspected animals at 31st Mobile Veterinary Section.	

-1-

WAR DIARY

of A.D.V.S., 19th Division.

INTELLIGENCE SUMMARY

(Erase heading not required.)

Instructions regarding War Diaries and Intelligence Summaries are contained in F.S. Regs., Part II. and the Staff Manual respectively. Title Pages will be prepared in manuscript.

Army Form C. 2118

Place	Date 1917.	Hour	Summary of Events and Information	Remarks and references to Appendices
COUIN.	Jany. 18.		Inspected D.H.Q. and Signal Coy.	
	19.		Weekly conference of Veterinary Officers at Office. Inspected No. 1 Section, D.A.C.	
	20.		Inspected 19th Divisional Train.	
	21.		Inspected 19th Divl. Signal Coy., and M.M.P.	
	22.		Inspected animals at M.V.S.	
	23.		Inspected D.H.Q. animals.	
	24.		Inspected horse of civilian with mange at COIGNEUX. Placed location "Out of Bounds".	
	25.		Inspected 88th Brigade, R.F.A.	
	26.		Weekly conference of Veterinary Officers at Office.	
	27.		Inspected 81st and 94th Field Coys., R.E.	
	28.		Inspected D.H.Q., Signal Coy., and M.M.P.	
	29.		Captain J.M.BROWN, A.V.C. returned from leave.	
	30.		Inspected H.Q., 86th Brigade, R.F.A.	
	31.		Inspected animals at 31st Mobile Veterinary Section.	
			* * * * * * *	
			Weather cold, with snow, during time in COUIN.	

Hasloone Moore
A.D.V.S.
19th Division

Army Form C. 2118

WAR DIARY
or
INTELLIGENCE SUMMARY

of A.D.V.S., 19th Division.

(Erase heading not required.)

Instructions regarding War Diaries and Intelligence Summaries are contained in F. S. Regs., Part II. and the Staff Manual respectively. Title Pages will be prepared in manuscript.

Place	Date 1917. Jany.	Hour	Summary of Events and Information	Remarks and references to Appendices
BERNAVILLE	1.		Inspected 19th Divisional Ammunition Column.	
	2.		Inspected 31st Mobile Veterinary Section.	
	3.		Inspected several Local Units.	
	4.		Inspected M.M.P. animals.	
	5.		Conference of Veterinary Officers at Office.	
	6.		D.D.V.S. inspected horses shod with sheet iron out of oil tins as preventative against P.U.N.	
	7.		Inspected 31st Mobile Veterinary Section.	
	8.		Inspected D.H.Q. and Signal Company.	
	9.		Moved to MARIEUX. 31st Mobile Vet. Section to AUTHIE.	
MARIEUX.	10.		Inspected local units.	
	11.		D.H.Q. moved to COUIN. Took over veterinary charge of 32nd Divisional Artillery, 7th Pontoon Park, 9th Labour Battalion, 37th Prisoners of War Company, 6th Cavalry Pioneers.	
COUIN.	12.		Conference of Veterinary Officers at office.	
	13.		Inspected 86th and 87th Brigades, R.F.A.	
	14.		Inspected 19th Divl. Signal Coy.	
	15.		Captain J.J.N.BROWN, A.V.C., left on leave. Inspected 7th Bn. Loyal North Lancs. Regt.	
	16.		32nd Divisional Artillery, except 223rd Field Coy., R.E., left area; also 6th Cav. Pioneers.	
	17.		Inspected animals, also 31st Mobile Veterinary Section.	

Army Form C. 2118

WAR DIARY
or
INTELLIGENCE SUMMARY   19th Division.
(Erase heading not required.)

Instructions regarding War Diaries and Intelligence Summaries are contained in F.S. Regs., Part II. and the Staff Manual respectively. Title Pages will be prepared in manuscript.

Place	Date	Hour	Summary of Events and Information	Remarks and references to Appendices
COUIN.	1917. Jany. 18.		Inspected D.H.Q. and Signal Coy.	
	19.		Weekly conference of Veterinary Officers at Office. Inspected No. 1 Section, D.A.C.	
	20.		Inspected 19th Divisional Train.	
	21.		Inspected 19th Divl. Signal Coy., and M.M.P.	
	22.		Inspected animals at M.V.S.	
	23.		Inspected D.H.Q. animals.	
	24.		Inspected horse of civilian with mange at COIGNEUX. Placed location "Out of Bounds".	
	25.		Inspected 88th Brigade, R.F.A.	
	26.		Weekly conference of Veterinary Officers at Office.	
	27.		Inspected 81st and 94th Field Coys., R.E.	
	28.		Inspected D.H.Q., Signal Coy.1 and M.M.P.	
	29.		Captain J.M.BROWN, A.V.C. returned from leave.	
	30.		Inspected H.Q., 86th Brigade, R.F.A.	
	31.		Inspected animals at 51st Mobile Veterinary Section.	
			* * * * * *	
			Weather cold, with snow, during time in COUIN.	

-2-

Jas Moore Major
A.D.V.S.
19 Division

Army Form C. 2118.

WAR DIARY of A.D.V.S., 19th Division.
INTELLIGENCE SUMMARY.

(Erase heading not required.)

Instructions regarding War Diaries and Intelligence Summaries are contained in F.S. Regs., Part II. and the Staff Manual respectively. Title pages will be prepared in manuscript.

Place	Date 1917	Hour	Summary of Events and Information	Remarks and references to Appendices
COUIN.	Feby. 1.		With D.D.V.S., 5th Army at 31st Mobile Veterinary Section. Inspected D/88th Bde., R.F.A.	
	2.		Inspected D/88th Bde., R.F.A. Conference of Veterinary Officers.	
	3.		Inspected B/88th Bde., R.F.A.	
	4.		Inspected 7th Pontoon Park and No. 1 Section D.A.C.	
	5.		Inspected B/88th Bde., R.F.A.	
	6.		Inspected 56th and 58th Infy. Bdes., 58 M.G.Coy., and 59th Field Ambulance.	
	7.		Inspected 86th (Army) Bde., R.F.A. Ammunition Column.	
	8.		Inspected 19th Divl. Signal Coy. and 87th Bde., R.F.A.	
	9.		Conference of Veterinary Officers at Office.	
	10.		Inspected 31st Mobile Vet. Section.	
	11.		Inspected 19th Divl. Signal Coy., and D/88th Bde., R.F.A.	
	12.		Inspected 88th Bde., R.F.A.	
	13.		Inspected 86th (Army) Bde., R.F.A.	
	14.		Inspected D/86th (Army) F.A.B. and Ammunition Column., also Section No. 2, D.A.C.	
	15.		Inspected Nos. 1 and 2 Sections D.A.C.	
	16.		Inspected 211 Field Coy., R.E. (31st Division). Conference of Veterinary Officers at Office.	
	17.		Inspected B/88th Bde., R.F.A.	

-1-

Army Form C. 2118.

WAR DIARY
of A.D.V.S.,
INTELLIGENCE SUMMARY. 19th Division.
(Erase heading not required.)

Instructions regarding War Diaries and Intelligence Summaries are contained in F. S. Regs., Part II. and the Staff Manual respectively. Title pages will be prepared in manuscript.

Place	Date 1917.	Hour	Summary of Events and Information	Remarks and references to Appendices
COUIN.	18.		Inspected B/88th Bde., R.F.A. and Signal Coy.	
	19.		Inspected No. 1 Sec., D.A.C., and B/88th Bde., R.F.A.	
	20.		Inspected D.H.Q. and M.M.P.	
	21.		31st Mobile Veterinary Section moved to BUS-LES-ARTOIS. Called on D.D.V.S. and V. Corps.	
	22.		Inspected 31st Mobile Veterinary Section.	
	23.		Inspected Ammunition Column and B/86th Bde., R.F.A. Confernce of Vet. Officers.	
	24.		Inspected 56th, 57th and 58th Infy. Bdes., M.G.Coys, and 5th Bn. South Wales Borderers.	
	25.		Inspected D.H.Q. and Signal Coy.	
	26.		Inspected 87th and 88th Bdes., R.F.A.	
	27.		Inspected D.A.C.	
	28.		Inspected 31st Mobile Veterinary Section.	
			* * * * * *	
			Weather very cold with heavy snow.	

Lashmore Major
A.D.V.S
19th Division

Army Form C. 2118.

WAR DIARY
or
INTELLIGENCE SUMMARY. 19th Division.
(Erase heading not required.)

Instructions regarding War Diaries and Intelligence Summaries are contained in F. S. Regs., Part II. and the Staff Manual respectively. Title pages will be prepared in manuscript.

Place	Date	Hour	Summary of Events and Information	Remarks and references to Appendices
COUIN.	1917 Feby. 1.		With D.D.V.S., 5th Army at 31st Mobile Veterinary Section. Inspected D/88th Bde., R.F.A.	
	2.		Inspected D/88th Bde., R.F.A. Conference of Veterinary Officers.	
	3.		Inspected B/88th Bde., R.F.A.	
	4.		Inspected 7th Pontoon Park and No. 1 Section D.A.C.	
	5.		Inspected B/88th Bde., R.F.A.	
	6.		Inspected 56th and 58th Infy. Bdes., 58 M.G.Coy., and 59th Field Ambulance.	
	7.		Inspected 86th (Army) Bde., R.F.A. Ammunition Column.	
	8.		Inspected 19th Divl. Signal Coy. and 87th Bde., R.F.A.	
	9.		Conference of Veterinary Officers at Office.	
	10.		Inspected 31st Mobile Vet. Section.	
	11.		Inspected 19th Divl. Signal Coy., and D/88th Bde., R.F.A.	
	12.		Inspected 88th Bde., R.F.A.	
	13.		Inspected 86th (Army) Bde., R.F.A.	
	14.		Inspected D/86th (Army) F.A.B. and Ammunition Column., also Section No. 2, D.A.C.	
	15.		Inspected Nos. 1 and 2 Sections D.A.C.	
	16.		Inspected 211 Field Coy., R.E. (31st Division). Conference of Veterinary Officers at Office.	
	17.		Inspected B/88th Bde., R.F.A.	

-1-

Army Form C. 2118.

WAR DIARY
of A.D.V.S.
INTELLIGENCE SUMMARY. 19th Division.

(Erase heading not required.)

Instructions regarding War Diaries and Intelligence Summaries are contained in F. S. Regs., Part II. and the Staff Manual respectively. Title pages will be prepared in manuscript.

Place	Date 1917.	Hour	Summary of Events and Information	Remarks and references to Appendices
COUIN.	18.		Inspected B/88th Bde., R.F.A. and Signal Coy.	
	19.		Inspected No. 1 Sec., D.A.C., and B/88th Bde., R.F.A.	
	20.		Inspected D.H.Q. and M.M.P.	
	21.		31st Mobile Veterinary Section moved to BUS-LES-ARTOIS. Called on D.D.V.S. and V. Corps.	
	22.		Inspected 31st Mobile Veterinary Section.	
	23.		Inspected Ammunition Column and B/86th Bde., R.F.A. Confernce of Vet. Officers.	
	24.		Inspected 56th, 57th and 58th Infy. Bdes., M.G.Coys, and 5th Bn. South Wales Borderers.	
	25.		Inspected D.H.Q. and Signal Coy.	
	26.		Inspected 87th and 88th Bdes., R.F.A.	
	27.		Inspected D.A.C.	
	28.		Inspected 31st Mobile Veterinary Section.	
			* * * * * *	
			Weather very cold with heavy snow.	

Jas Moore Maj AVC
A.D.V.S.
19th Division

Army Form C. 2118

WAR DIARY

of A.D.V.S., 19th Division.

INTELLIGENCE SUMMARY

(Erase heading not required.)

Instructions regarding War Diaries and Intelligence Summaries are contained in F.S. Regs., Part II. and the Staff Manual respectively. Title Pages will be prepared in manuscript.

Place	Date 1917.	Hour	Summary of Events and Information	Remarks and references to Appendices
COUIN.	March 1.		Inspected D.H.Q. and Signals.	
	2.		Weekly conference of Veterinary Officers at Office.	
	3.		Inspected 19th Divisional Train.	
	4.		Left COUIN, arrived BUS LES ARTOIS.	
BUS LES ARTOIS.	5.		Inspected Nos. 1 and 2 Sections, D.A.C.	
	6.		Inspected 82nd Field Coy., R.E.	
	7.		Inspected 87th and 88th Bdes., R.F.A.	
	8.		Inspected 31st Mobile Veterinary Section.	
	9.		D.D.V.S. and D.D.R., Fifth Army called. Weekly conference of Veterinary Officers at Office.	
	10.		Left BUS for BEAUVAL. Inspected 9th Bn. Cheshire Regt. and 5th Bn. S.W.Borderers (Pioneers).	
BEAUVAL.	11.		Left BEAUVAL for BOQUEMAISON.	
BOQUEMAISON	12.		Inspected local units.	
	13.		Left BOQUEMAISON for RAMECOURT.	
RAMECOURT.	14.		Left RAMECOURT for PERNES. Inspected Signal Coy., and 5/S.W.B.	
PERNES.	15.		Inspected 5/S.W.B. (P).	
	16.		Left PERNES for NORRENT FONTES.	

-1-

Army Form C. 2118

WAR DIARY
INTELLIGENCE SUMMARY
for A.D.V.S., 19th Division.

(Erase heading not required.)

Instructions regarding War Diaries and Intelligence Summaries are contained in F.S. Regs., Part II. and the Staff Manual respectively. Title Pages will be prepared in manuscript.

Place	Date 1917	Hour	Summary of Events and Information	Remarks and references to Appendices
NORRENT FONTES.	March 17.		Inspected Units in vicinity.	
	18.		Left NORRENT FONTES for STEENBECQUE.	
STEENBECQUE	19		D.D.V.S., Second Army called. Left STEENBECQUE for MERRIS.	
MERRIS.	20.		Left MERRIS for FLETRE.	
FLETRE.	21.		Inspected D.A.C.	
	22.		Inspected S.W.B., 58 Machine Gun Coy., 9th Bn. Cheshire Regiment.	
	23.		Inspected 51st Mobile Veterinary Section.	
	24.		Inspected D.H.Q. and Signal Coy.,	
	25.		Inspected 87th Brigade, R.F.A.	
	26.		Inspected D.A.C.	
	27.		Inspected M.M.P.	
	28.		Inspected Units of 57th Infy. Bde.	
	29.		Weekly conference of Veterinary Officers at Office.	
	30.		Inspected D.A.C.	
	31.		Left FLETRE for WESTOUTRE.	

-2-

WAR DIARY

of A.D.V.S., 19th Division.

INTELLIGENCE SUMMARY

(Erase heading not required.)

Army Form C. 2118

Instructions regarding War Diaries and Intelligence Summaries are contained in F.S. Regs., Part II. and the Staff Manual respectively. Title Pages will be prepared in manuscript.

Place	Date 1917.	Hour	Summary of Events and Information	Remarks and references to Appendices
COUIN.	March 1.		Inspected D.H.Q. and Signals.	
	2.		Weekly conference of Veterinary Officers at Office.	
	3.		Inspected 19th Divisional Train.	
	4.		Left COUIN, arrived BUS LES ARTOIS.	
BUS LES ARTOIS.	5.		Inspected Nos. 1 and 2 Sections, D.A.C.	
	6.		Inspected 82nd Field Coy., R.E.	
	7.		Inspected 87th and 88th Bdes., R.F.A.	
	8.		Inspected 31st Mobile Veterinary Section.	
	9.		D.D.V.S. and D.D.R., Fifth Army called. Weekly conference of Veterinary Officers at Office.	
	10.		Left BUS for BEAUVAL. Inspected 9th Bn. Cheshire Regt. and 5th Bn. S.W.Borderers (Pioneers).	
BEAUVAL.	11.		Left BEAUVAL for BOQUEMAISON.	
BOQUEMAISON	12.		Inspected local units.	
	13.		Left BOQUEMAISON for RAMECOURT.	
RAMECOURT	14.		Left RAMECOURT for PERNES. Inspected Signal Coy., and 5/S.W.B.	
PERNES.	15.		Inspected 5/S.W.B. (P).	
	16.		Left PERNES for NORRENT FONTES.	

-1-

Army Form C. 2118

WAR DIARY

INTELLIGENCE SUMMARY

for A.D.V.S., 19th Division.

(Erase heading not required.)

Instructions regarding War Diaries and Intelligence Summaries are contained in F. S. Regs., Part II. and the Staff Manual respectively. Title Pages will be prepared in manuscript.

Place	Date 1917.	Hour	Summary of Events and Information	Remarks and references to Appendices
NORRENT FONTES.	March 17.		Inspected Units in vicinity.	
	18.		Left NORRENT FONTES for STEENBECQUE.	
STEENBECQUE	19		D.D.V.S., Second Army called. Left STEENBECQUE for MERRIS.	
MERRIS.	20.		Left MERRIS for FLETRE.	
FLETRE.	21.		Inspected D.A.C.	
	22.		Inspected S.W.B., 58 Machine Gun Coy., 9th Bn. Cheshire Regiment.	
	23.		Inspected 31st Mobile Veterinary Section.	
	24.		Inspected D.H.Q. and Signal Coy.,	
	25.		Inspected 87th Brigade, R.F.A.	
	26.		Inspected D.A.C.	
	27.		Inspected M.M.P.	
	28.		Inspected Units of 57th Infy. Bde.	
	29.		Weekly conference of Veterinary Officers at Office.	
	30.		Inspected D.A.C.	
	31.		Left FLETRE for WESTOUTRE.	

WAR DIARY of A.D.V.S., 19th Division.

INTELLIGENCE SUMMARY

Army Form C. 2118

Instructions regarding War Diaries and Intelligence Summaries are contained in F.S. Regs., Part II. and the Staff Manual respectively. Title Pages will be prepared in manuscript.

Place	Date 1917.	Hour	Summary of Events and Information	Remarks and references to Appendices
April WESTOUTRE.	1.		Inspected 19th Signal Coy.,	
	2.		Inspected 58th Infy. Bde.	
	3.		Inspected 5th South Wales Borderers (Pioneers).	
	4.		Inspected 19th D.A.C.	
	5.		D.D.V.S., 2nd Army called.	
	6.		Conference of Veterinary Officers at Office.	
	7.		Inspected 56th Infy. Bde.	
	8.		Inspected 7/N.Lan. R. and Divl. Train, A.S.C.	
	9.		Inspected 88th Bde., R.F.A.	
	10.		Inspected local units.	
	11.		Inspected 5th South Wales Borderers, 81st and 94th Field Coys., R.E. and 7/E.Lan. R.	
	12.		Inspected Signal Coy.	
	13.		Conference of Veterinary Officers at Office.	
	14.		Inspected 9/Welsh, 9/Cheshire, and 7/N.Lan. Regts.	
	15.		Inspected local units.	
	16.		Inspected 7/R.Lancs. R., 7/N.Lan. R. and 5/S.Wales Bord. (P).	
	17.		Inspected Signal Coy.	
	18.		Inspected several small units in locality.	

-1-

WAR DIARY

INTELLIGENCE SUMMARY

of A.D.V.S., 19th Division.

Army Form C. 2118

Instructions regarding War Diaries and Intelligence Summaries are contained in F.S. Regs., Part II. and the Staff Manual respectively. Title Pages will be prepared in manuscript.

(Erase heading not required.)

Place	Date 1917.	Hour	Summary of Events and Information	Remarks and references to Appendices
WESTOUTRE	April 19.		Routine work.	
	20.		Conference of Veterinary Officers at Office.	
	21.		Inspected 10/Worc., 10/R.War., 8/Glouc., 8/N.Staff. Regts. and 57 Coy., M.G.Corps.	
	22.		Inspected Divl. Train, A.S.C.	
	23.		Inspected Signal Coy.	
	24.		Inspected 5/S.Wales Borderers (P).	
	25.		Inspected 82nd Field Coy., R.E.	
	26.		Inspected 56th and 57th Infy. Bdes.	
	27.		Inspected Signal Coy. Weekly conference at Office.	
	28.		Inspected 87th Bde. R.F.A.	
	29.		Routine work.	
	30.		Inspected site for M.V.S. in POPERINGHE AREA.	

Army Form C. 2118

WAR DIARY
or
INTELLIGENCE SUMMARY
of A.D.V.S., 19th Division.

(Erase heading not required.)

Instructions regarding War Diaries and Intelligence Summaries are contained in F. S. Regs., Part II. and the Staff Manual respectively. Title Pages will be prepared in manuscript.

Place	Date	Hour	Summary of Events and Information	Remarks and references to Appendices
April WESTOUTRE.	1917. 1.		Inspected 19th Signal Coy.,	
	2.		Inspected 58th Infy. Bde.	
	3.		Inspected 5th South Wales Borderers (Pioneers).	
	4.		Inspected 19th D.A.C.	
	5.		D.D.V.S., 2nd Army called.	
	6.		Conference of Veterinary Officers at Office.	
	7.		Inspected 56th Infy. Bde.	
	8.		Inspected 7/N.Lan. R. and Divl. Train, A.S.C.	
	9.		Inspected 88th Bde., R.F.A.	
	10.		Inspected local units.	
	11.		Inspected 5th South Wales Borderers, 81st and 94th Field Coys., R.E. and 7/E.Lan. R.	
	12.		Inspected Signal Coy.	
	13.		Conference of Veterinary Officers at Office.	
	14.		Inspected 9/Welsh, 9/Cheshire, and 9/N.Lan. Regts.	
	15.		Inspected local units.	
	16.		Inspected 7/R.Lancs. R., 7/N.Lan. R. and 5/S.Wales Bord. (P).	
	17.		Inspected Signal Coy.	
	18.		Inspected several small units in locality.	

-1-

Army Form C. 2118

WAR DIARY
or
INTELLIGENCE SUMMARY
of A.D.V.S., 19th Division.
(Erase heading not required.)

Instructions regarding War Diaries and Intelligence Summaries are contained in F.S. Regs., Part II. and the Staff Manual respectively. Title Pages will be prepared in manuscript.

Place	Date	Hour	Summary of Events and Information	Remarks and references to Appendices
WESTOUTRE	1917. April 19.		Routine work.	
	20.		Conference of Veterinary Officers at Office.	
	21.		Inspected 10/Worc., 10/R.War., 8/Glouc., 8/N.Staff. Regts. and 57 Coy., M.G.Corps.	
	22.		Inspected Divl. Train, A.S.C.	
	23.		Inspected Signal Coy.	
	24.		Inspected 5/S.Wales Borderers (P).	
	25.		Inspected 82nd Field Coy., R.E.	
	26.		Inspected 56th and 57th Infy. Bdes.	
	27.		Inspected Signal Coy. Weekly conference at Office.	
	28.		Inspected 87th Bde. R.F.A.	
	29.		Routine work.	
	30.		Inspected site for M.V.S. in POPERINGHE AREA.	

Army Form C. 2118

WAR DIARY

INTELLIGENCE SUMMARY

of A.D.V.S., 19th Division.

(Erase heading not required.)

Instructions regarding War Diaries and Intelligence Summaries are contained in F.S. Regs., Part II. and the Staff Manual respectively. Title Pages will be prepared in manuscript.

Place	Date 1917.	Hour	Summary of Events and Information	Remarks and references to Appendices
WESTOUTRE.	May 1		Routine work.	
	2		Office and Mobile vet. Sec moved to BUSSEBOOM.	
BUSSEBOOM.	3		Inspected 6/Wilts. R., 7/N.Lan.R. and 7/R.Lanc. R.	
	4		Routine work.	
	5		Inspected D.H.Q. animals. Called on A.D.V.S., 41st Division.	
	6		Routine work.	
	7		Inspected local units.	
	8		Inspected 9/Welsh R.	
	9		Routine work.	
	10		Inspected No. 3 Section, D.A.C., M.M.P. and Signal Coy.	
	11		Mobile Vet. Sec. moved to WESTOUTRE.	
	12		Office moved with D.H.Q. to WESTOUTRE.	
WESTOUTRE.	13		Local inspections and routine work.	
	14		Inspected 56th Infy. Bde. and 56 Coy., M.G.Corps.	
	15		Inspected 57th Infy. Bde. and 57 Coy., M.G.Corps.	
	16		Inspected 5/S.Wales Bord. (P).	
	17		Routine work.	

-1-

1875 Wt. W593/826 1,000,000 4/15 J.B.C. & A. A.D.S.S./Forms/C. 2118.

Army Form C. 2118

WAR DIARY of A.D.V.S., 19th Division.
INTELLIGENCE SUMMARY
(Erase heading not required.)

Instructions regarding War Diaries and Intelligence Summaries are contained in F.S. Regs., Part II. and the Staff Manual respectively. Title Pages will be prepared in manuscript.

Place	Date 1917	Hour	Summary of Events and Information	Remarks and references to Appendices
WESTOUTRE	May 18		On leave.	
	28		Returned from leave.	
	29		Inspected 19th Signal Coy. and 150th (Army) F.A.B.	
	30		Inspected 56 Coy., M.G.Corps., 58th Infy. Bde., and 58 Coy., M.G.Corps.	
	31		Routine work.	
			************	
			The weather has been fine and warm.	

Eastoon Maj. A.V.C.
A.D.V.S. 19 Division

-2-

1875 Wt. W593/826 1,000,000 4/15 J.B.C. & A. A.D.S.S./Forms/C. 2118.

Army Form C. 2118

WAR DIARY
INTELLIGENCE SUMMARY of A.D.V.S., 19th Division.

(Erase heading not required.)

Instructions regarding War Diaries and Intelligence Summaries are contained in F. S. Regs., Part II. and the Staff Manual respectively. Title Pages will be prepared in manuscript.

Place	Date 1917.	Hour	Summary of Events and Information	Remarks and references to Appendices
WESTOUTRE.	May 1		Routine work.	
	2		Office and Mobile Vet. Sec moved to BUSSEBOOM.	
BUSSEBOOM.	3		Inspected 6/Wilts. R., 7/N.Lan.R. and 7/R.Lanc. R.	
	4		Routine work.	
	5		Inspected D.H.Q. animals. Called on A.D.V.S., 41st Division.	
	6		Routine work.	
	7		Inspected local units.	
	8		Inspected 9/Welsh R.	
	9		Routine work.	
	10		Inspected No. 3 Section, D.A.C., M.M.P. and Signal Coy.	
	11		Mobile Vet. Sec. moved to WESTOUTRE.	
	12		Office moved with D.H.Q. to WESTOUTRE.	
WESTOUTRE.	13		Local inspections and routine work.	
	14		Inspected 56th Infy. Bde. and 56 Coy., M.G.Corps.	
	15		Inspected 57th Infy. Bde. and 57 Coy., M.G.Corps.	
	16		Inspected 5/S.Wales Bord. (P).	
	17		Routine work.	

-1-

Army Form C. 2118

WAR DIARY

of A.D.V.S., 19th Division.

INTELLIGENCE SUMMARY

(Erase heading not required.)

Instructions regarding War Diaries and Intelligence Summaries are contained in F.S. Regs., Part II. and the Staff Manual respectively. Title Pages will be prepared in manuscript.

Place	Date 1917	Hour	Summary of Events and Information	Remarks and references to Appendices
WESTOUTRE	May 18		On leave.	
	28		Returned from leave.	
	29		Inspected 19th Signal Coy. and 150th (Army) F.A.B.	
	30		Inspected 56 Coy., M.G.Corps., 58th Infy. Bde., and 58 Coy., M.G.Corps.	
	31		Routine work.	
			************	
			The weather has been fine and warm.	

J. Ashton Major A.V.C.
A.D.V.S
19 Division

Army Form C. 2118.

WAR DIARY
of A.D.V.S., 19th Division.
INTELLIGENCE SUMMARY.
(Erase heading not required.)

Instructions regarding War Diaries and Intelligence Summaries are contained in F.S. Regs., Part II. and the Staff Manual respectively. Title pages will be prepared in manuscript.

Place	Date	Hour	Summary of Events and Information	Remarks and references to Appendices
WESTOUTRE.	1917. June 1.		Weekly conference of Veterinary Officers at Office.	
	2.		Inspected 87th and 88th Brigades, R.F.A.	
	3.		Inspected 150th A.F.A. Bde. Selected animals for skin desease.	
	4.		Inspected Mobile Veterinary Section.	
	5.		Inspected D.H.Q., M.M.P., and 19th Sig. Coy.	
	6.		Hostile aircraft dropped bombs in wagon lines of 250 A.F.A. Bde., killing 32 and wounding 30 animals. Inspected 56th Infy. Bde.	
	7.		Local inspections.	
	8.		Conference at Office. Inspected 87th Bde., R.F.A.	
	9.		Routine work.	
	10.		Inspections of attached units.	
	11.		Inspected 150th A.F.A. Bde., 5/S.Wales Bord. (P)., and 19th Divl. Sig. Coy.&rd S/W Staff.R.	
	12.		Inspected 10/Worc. R.	
	13.		Routine work.	
	14.		31st Mob. Vet. Sec. moved to M.23.c.6.2. (Locre). Inspected 59th Field Ambulance.	
	15.		Weekly conference of Veterinary Officers	
	16.		Inspected 19th Divl	

-1-

Army Form C. 2118.

WAR DIARY
or
INTELLIGENCE SUMMARY. of A.D.V.S. 19th Division.
(Erase heading not required.)

Instructions regarding War Diaries and Intelligence Summaries are contained in F. S. Regs., Part II. and the Staff Manual respectively. Title pages will be prepared in manuscript.

Place	Date 1917. June.	Hour	Summary of Events and Information	Remarks and references to Appendices
WESTOUTRE.	17.		Took over IX Corps Dip. Inspected site for Mob. Vet. Sec. at ST JAN'S CAPPEL.	
	18.		Captain S.S. KERR, A.V.C., returned from sick leave. Inspected 58th Inf. Bde.	
	19.		Office moved to ST JAN'S CAPPEL. 51st Mob.Vet.Sec. to ST JAN'S CAPPEL-BAILLEUL Road.	
	20.		Inspection of wallets of Sergeants, A.V.C. and others at M.V.S. Attended conference of D.V.S. at ST OMER.	
ST JAN'S CAPPEL.	21.		Inspected D.H.Q., M.M.P. and Signal Coy.	
	22.		Weekly conference at Office.	
	23.		Inspected 9/R.W.Fus.	
	24.		Local inspections.	
	25.		Inspected Sig. Coy. and 7/S.Lan.R.	
	26.		Inspected 10/R.War.R.	
	27.		Inspected C/88th Bde., R.F.A. especially for skin desease.	
	28.		Routine work.	
	29.		Captain A.R.SMYTHE, O.C., 51st Mob. Vet. Sec. left on leave. Weekly conference at Office.	
	30.		Inspected C/315 A.F.A. Bde. for skin desease. Inspected 51st Mob. Vet. Sec. and local units. Weather fair.	

H.S. Moore Major A.V.C.
D.A.D.V.S. 19th Division

Army Form C. 2118.

WAR DIARY
of
INTELLIGENCE SUMMARY. 19th Division.
A.D.V.S.

(Erase heading not required.)

Instructions regarding War Diaries and Intelligence Summaries are contained in F. S. Regs., Part II. and the Staff Manual respectively. Title pages will be prepared in manuscript.

Place	Date	Hour	Summary of Events and Information	Remarks and references to Appendices
WESTOUTRE	1917. June 1.		Weekly conference of Veterinary Officers at Office.	
	2.		Inspected 87th and 88th Brigades, R.F.A.	
	3.		Inspected 150th A.F.A. Bde. Selected animals for skin desease.	
	4.		Inspected Mobile Veterinary Section.	
	5.		Inspected D.H.Q., M.M.P., and 19th Sig. Coy.	
	6.		Hostile aircraft dropped bombs in wagon lines of 150 A.F.A. Bde, killing 32 and wounding 30 animals. Inspected 56th Infy. Bde.	
	7.		Local inspections.	
	8.		Conference at Office. Inspected 87th Bde., R.F.A.	
	9.		Routine work.	
	10.		Inspections of attached units.	
	11.		Inspected 150th A.F.A. Bde., S/S.Wales Bord. (P)., and 19th Divl. Sig. Coy.and 8/N.Staff.R.	
	12.		Inspected 10/Worc.R.	
	13.		Routine work.	
	14.		31st Mob. Vet. Sec. moved to M.23.c.6.2. (Locre). Inspected 59th Field Ambulance.	
	15.		Weekly conference of Veterinary Officers.	
	16.		Inspected 19th	

-1-

Army Form C. 2118.

WAR DIARY

of A.D.V.S.,

INTELLIGENCE SUMMARY. 19th Division.

(Erase heading not required.)

Instructions regarding War Diaries and Intelligence Summaries are contained in F. S. Regs. Part II. and the Staff Manual respectively. Title pages will be prepared in manuscript.

Place	Date 1917.	Hour	Summary of Events and Information	Remarks and references to Appendices
WESTOUTRE.	June 17.		Took over IX Corps Dip. Inspected site for Mob. Vet. Sec. at ST JAN'S CAPPEL.	
	18.		Captain S.S. KERR, A.V.C., returned from sick leave. Inspected 58th Infy. Bde.	
	19.		Office moved to St JAN'S CAPPEL. 31st Mob. Vet. Sec. to ST JAN'S CAPPEL-BAILLEUL Road.	
ST JAN'S CAPPEL.	20.		Inspection of wallets of Sergeants, A.V.C. and others at M.V.S. Attended conference of D.V.S. at ST OMER.	
	21.		Inspected D.H.Q., M.M.P. and Signal Coy.	
	22.		Weekly conference at Office.	
	23.		Inspected 9/R.W.Fus.	
	24.		Local inspections.	
	25.		Inspected Sig. Coy. and 7/S.Lan.R.	
	26.		Inspected 10/R.War.R.	
	27.		Inspected C/88th Bde., R.F.A. especially for skin desease.	
	28.		Routine work.	
	29.		Captain A.R.SMYTHE, O.C. 31st Mob. Vet. Sec. left on leave. Weekly conference at Office.	
	30.		Inspected C/315 A.F.A. Bde. for skin desease. Inspected 31st Mob. Vet. Sec. and local units.	
			Weather fair.	

F.S. Moore Major A.V.C.
A.D.V.S. 19 Division

-2-

Army Form C. 2118.

WAR DIARY
of A.D.V.S., 19th Division.
INTELLIGENCE SUMMARY.

(Erase heading not required.)

Instructions regarding War Diaries and Intelligence Summaries are contained in F. S. Regs., Part II. and the Staff Manual respectively. Title pages will be prepared in manuscript.

Place	Date 1917	Hour	Summary of Events and Information	Remarks and references to Appendices
ST JAN'S CAPPEL.	July 1.		Routine work.	
	2.		31st Mobile Veterinary Section removed to LOCRE. C/88th Bde. R.F.A. attached Second Army School left Area.	
	3.		Moved Office to Dug-out, south side of SCHERPENBERG.	
SCHERPENBERG	4.		Inspected 5/S.Wales Bord. and 7/S.Lan. R.	
	5.		Inspected 87th and 88th Bde., R.F.A., 7/E.Lan. R. and 56 M.G.Coy.	
	6.		Weekly conference of Veterinary Officers at Office.	
	7.		Inspected 81st and 94th Field Coys., R.E., 58th Infy. Bde. and 56 M.G.Coy.	
	8.		Inspected 88th Bde., R.F.A.	
	9.		Captain A.R.SMYTHE, A.V.C., returned from leave. Inspected 7/N.Lan.R., N.M.P. and D.H.Q.	
	10.		Inspected 57th Infy. Bde. and 57 M.G.Coy.	
	11.		Lieut. H.W.STEVENS, A.V.C. left this Division to take over veterinary charge of X Corps Heavy Artillery. Inspected Signal Company.	
	12.		Inspected 9/Welsh R.	
	13.		Weekly conference at Office.	
	14.		Inspected 87th Bde., R.F.A.	
	15.		Inspected 94th Field Coy., R.E. & D.R. & LE.	

Army Form C. 2118.

WAR DIARY
of D.A.D.V.S., 19th Division.
INTELLIGENCE SUMMARY.
(Erase heading not required.)

Instructions regarding War Diaries and Intelligence Summaries are contained in F. S. Regs., Part II. and the Staff Manual respectively. Title pages will be prepared in manuscript.

Place	Date 1917	Hour	Summary of Events and Information	Remarks and references to Appendices
SCHERPENBERG	July 16.		Inspection of units with A.D.V.S., IX Corps. Inspected 87th Bde., R.F.A., 81st Field Coy., R.E., and 58th Infy. Bde.	
	17.		Inspected Signal Coy.	
	18.		Inspected 88th Bde., R.F.A.	
	19.		Inspected D.H.Q. and M.M.P.	
	20.		Captain T. MENZIES left on leave. Weekly conference of Vet. Officers. Inspected 246 Coy., Machine Gun Corps, 5/S.Wales Bord. and 82nd Field Coy., R.E. Malleined animals of 246 Coy., M.G.Corps.	
	21.		Routine work.	
	22.		Routine work and local inspections.	
	23.		Inspections with A.D.V.S. IX Corps, D.A.C., 245 Coy. M.G.Corps. 31st M.V.S. bombed by hostile aircraft. One attached man killed, one fatally wounded and one A.S.C. driver attached wounded. Four animals killed and 11 wounded.	
	24.		Inspected D.H.Q. and M.M.P.	
	25.		Routine work. Inspected Signal Coy.	
	26.		Member of Board for selection of brood mares. Inspected 81st, 82nd and 94th Field Coys. R.E.	
	27.		All vet. Officers attended at Office. Inspected 87th, 88th Bdes., R.F.A. and D.A.C. with members of Board.	
	28.		Inspected Nos. 2 and 3 Secs., D.A.C., 59th Field Amb., 56th and 57th Bdes.	
	29.		Inspections and routine work.	

-2-

Army Form C. 2118.

WAR DIARY
or
INTELLIGENCE SUMMARY

A.D.M.S., 19th Division.

(Erase heading not required.)

Place	Date	Hour	Summary of Events and Information	Remarks and references to Appendices
	1917 July.			
	30		Inspected 57th Field Ambulance, D.H.Q., Divisional Train, 58th Infy. Bde. and Sig. Coy.	
	31.		Routine work.	

-3-

Army Form C. 2118.

WAR DIARY
of D.A.D.V.S.,
INTELLIGENCE SUMMARY 19th Division.
(Erase heading not required.)

Instructions regarding War Diaries and Intelligence Summaries are contained in F. S. Regs., Part II. and the Staff Manual respectively. Title pages will be prepared in manuscript.

Place	Date 1917	Hour	Summary of Events and Information	Remarks and references to Appendices
ST JAN'S CAPPELL.	July 1.		Routine work.	
	2.		31st Mobile Veterinary Section removed to LOCRE. C/88th Bde. R.F.A. attached Second Army School left Area. Inspected 19th Signal Coy.	
	3.		Moved Office to Dug-out, south side of SCHERPENBERG.	
SCHERPENBERG	4.		Inspected 5/S.Wales Bord. and 7/S.Lan.R.	
	5.		Inspected 87th and 88th Bdes., R.F.A., 7/E.Lan.R. and 56 M.G.Coy.	
	6.		Weekly conference of Veterinary Officers at Office.	
	7.		Inspected 81st and 94th Field Coys., R.E., 58th Infy. Bde. and 56 M.G.Coy.	
	8.		Inspected 88th Bde., R.F.A.	
	9.		Captain A.R.SMYTHE, A.V.C. returned from leave. Inspected 7/N.Lan.R., M.M.P. and D.H.Q.	
	10.		Inspected 57th Infy. Bde. and 57 M.G.Coy.	
	11.		Lieut. H.W.STEVENS, A.V.C. left this Division to take over veterinary charge of X Corps Heavy Artillery. Inspected Signal Company.	
	12.		Inspected 9/Welsh R.	
	13.		Weekly conference at Office.	
	14.		Inspected 87th Bde., R.F.A.	
	15.		Inspected 94th Field Coy., R.E.	

Army Form C. 2118.

WAR DIARY
or
INTELLIGENCE SUMMARY.

19th Division.

(Erase heading not required.)

Instructions regarding War Diaries and Intelligence Summaries are contained in F. S. Regs., Part II. and the Staff Manual respectively. Title pages will be prepared in manuscript.

Place	Date 1917	Hour	Summary of Events and Information	Remarks and references to Appendices
SCHERPENBERG	July 16		Inspection of units with A.D.V.S., IX Corps. Inspected 87th Bde., R.F.A., 81st Field Coy., R.E., and 58th Infy. Bde.	
	17.		Inspected Signal Coy.	
	18.		Inspected 88th Bde., R.F.A.	
	19.		Inspected D.H.Q. and M.M.P.	
	20.		Captain T. MENZIES left on leave. Weekly conference of Vet. Officers. Inspected 245 Coy., Machine Gun Corps, 5/S.Wales Bord. and 82nd Field Coy., R.E. Malleined animals of 246 Coy., M.G.Corps.	
	21.		Routine work.	
	22.		Routine work and local inspections.	
	23.		Inspections with A.D.V.S., IX Corps, D.A.C., 246 Coy., M.G.Corps. 31st M.V.S. bombed by hostile aircraft. One attached man killed, one fatally wounded and one A.S.C. driver attached wounded. Four animals killed and 11 wounded.	
	24.		Inspected D.H.Q. and M.M.P.	
	25.		Routine work. Inspected Signal Coy.	
	26.		Member of Board for selection of brood mares. Inspected 81st, 82nd and 94th Field Coys. R.E.	
	27.		All vet. officers attended at office. Inspected 87th, 88th Bdes., R.F.A. and D.A.C. with members of Board.	
	28.		Inspected Nos. 2 and 3 Secs., D.A.C., 59th Field Amb., 56th and 57th Bdes.	
	29.		Inspections and routine work.	

-2-

Army Form C. 2118.

WAR DIARY
of D.A.D.V.S., 19th Division.
INTELLIGENCE SUMMARY
(Erase heading not required.)

Instructions regarding War Diaries and Intelligence Summaries are contained in F. S. Regs., Part II. and the Staff Manual respectively. Title pages will be prepared in manuscript.

Place	Date 1917	Hour	Summary of Events and Information	Remarks and references to Appendices
	July. 30		Inspected 57th Field Ambulance, D.H.Q., Divisional Train, 58th Infy. Bde. and Sig. Coy.	
	31.		Routine work.	

Army Form C. 2118.

WAR DIARY
*** INTELLIGENCE*** SUMMARY

of D.A.D.V.S., 19th Division.

(Erase heading not required.)

Instructions regarding War Diaries and Intelligence Summaries are contained in F. S. Regs., Part II. and the Staff Manual respectively. Title pages will be prepared in manuscript.

Place	Date	Hour	Summary of Events and Information	Remarks and references to Appendices
	1917 Aug.			
SCHERPENBERG	1.		Routine work.	
	2.		Inspected Signal Coy.	
	3.		Conference of Veterinary Officers at Office.	
	4.		Called on A.D.V.S., IX Corps. Inspected M.M.P.	
	5.		Inspected, with A.D.V.S., IX Corps, horse dip.	
	6.		Acting A.D.V.S., IX Corps during absence of Lt-Col. Bartlett on leave.	
	7.		Inspected 315 (A) B.A.C.	
	8.		Visited horse dip, Remount Depot and IX Corps M.V.D. Division moved to ST JAN'S CAPPEL.	
ST JAN'S CAPPEL	9.		Visited ~~Divisies~~ horse dip. 31st Mobile Vet. Sec. left for LUMBRES.	
	10.		D.D.V.S. called. Selected site for IX Corps M.V.D. and called at dip. D.H.Q. left for LUMBRES.	
LUMBRES.	11.		Inspected A/87th Bde., R.F.A.	
	12.		Visited horse dip and Mobile Veterinary Section of 30th Division.	
	13.		Inspected 37th Division Mob. Vet. Sec., horse dip and No. 1 Sec. 19th D.A.C.	
	14.		Visited dip. Inspected 30th and 28th Divl. M.V.Sections.	
	15.		Inspected 87th Bde. R.F.A.	
	16.		Visited Horse Dip and IX Corps M.V.D.	

-1-

D.A.D.V.S.
Army Form ~~C. 2118.~~

WAR DIARY
of D.A.D.V.S., 19th Division.
~~INTELLIGENCE~~ SUMMARY

(Erase heading not required.)

Instructions regarding War Diaries and Intelligence Summaries are contained in F. S. Regs., Part II. and the Staff Manual respectively. Title pages will be prepared in manuscript.

Place	Date 1917	Hour	Summary of Events and Information	Remarks and references to Appendices
LUMBRES.	Aug. 17.		Left IX Corps for LUMBRES on return of Lieut.-Col. Bartlett from leave.	
	18.		Routine work.	
	19.		Inspected D.H.Q.	
	20.		Inspected 81st Field Coy., R.E. and Signal Company.	
	21.		Inspected 9th Royal Welsh Fusiliers.	
	22.		Inspected 15th Reserve Park, A.S.C.	
	23.		Inspected local units.	
	24.		Inspected D.H.Q.	
	25.		Routine work and inspections.	
	26.		Routine work.	
	27.		Inspected 81st Field Coy., R.E.	
	28.		31st Mobile Veterinary Section left for ST JAN'S CAPPEL by road.	
	29.		Moved to ST JAN'S CAPPEL.	
ST JANS CAPPEL	30.		Inspected Signal Coy.	
	31.		Inspected 58th and 59th Field Ambulances, 6th Wilts. R., H.Q., 58th Infy. Bde.	

Signature D.A.D.V.S. 19th Division

A6945 Wt. W14422/M1160 350,000 12/16 D. D. & L. Forms/C/2118/14.

Army Form C. 2118.

WAR DIARY
or
INTELLIGENCE SUMMARY

(Erase heading not required.)

D.D.V.S., 19th Division.

Place	Date	Hour	Summary of Events and Information	Remarks and references to Appendices
	1917 Aug.			
SCHERPENBERG	1.		Routine work.	
	2.		Inspected Signal Coy.	
	3.		Conference of Veterinary Officers at Office.	
	4.		Called on A.D.V.S., IX Corps. Inspected M.M.P.	
	5.		Inspected, with A.D.V.S., IX Corps, horse dip.	
	6.		Acting A.D.V.S., IX Corps during absence of Lt.-Col. Bartlett on leave.	
	7.		Inspected 315 (A) B.A.C.	
	8.		Visited horse-dip, Remount Depot and IX Corps M.V.D. Division moved to ST JAN'S CAPPEL.	
ST JAN'S CAPPEL	9.		Visited Divisional horse dip. 31st Mobile Vet. Sec. left for LUMBRES.	
	10.		D.D.V.S. called. Selected site for IX Corps M.V.D. and called at dip. D.H.Q. left for LUMBRES.	
LUMBRES.	11.		Inspected A/87th Bde., R.F.A.	
	12.		Visited horse dip and Mobile Veterinary Section of 30th Division.	
	13.		Inspected 37th Division Mob. Vet. Sec., horse dip and No. 1 Sec. 19th D.A.C.	
	14.		Visited dip. Inspected 30th and 28th Divl. M.V.Sections.	
	15.		Inspected 87th Bde. R.F.A.	
	16.		Visited Horse/Mule dip IX Corps	

-1-

Army Form C.2118.
19TH DIVISION.
No.................
Date............

WAR DIARY
or
INTELLIGENCE SUMMARY
(Erase heading not required.)

19th Division.

Place	Date	Hour	Summary of Events and Information	Remarks and references to Appendices
LUMBRES.	1917. Aug. 17.		Left IX Corps for LUMBRES on return of Lieut-Col. Bartlett from leave.	
	18.		Routine work.	
	19.		Inspected D.H.Q.	
	20.		Inspected 81st Field Coy., R.E. and Signal Company.	
	21.		Inspected 9th Royal Welsh Fusiliers.	
	22.		Inspected 15th Reserve Park, A.S.C.	
	23.		Inspected local units.	
	24.		Inspected D.H.Q.	
	25.		Routine work and inspections.	
	26.		Routine work.	
	27.		Inspected 81st Field Coy., R.E.	
	28.		31st Mobile Veterinary Section left for ST JAN'S CAPPEL by road.	
	29.		Moved to ST JAN'S CAPPEL.	
ST JANS CAPPEL	30.		Inspected Signal Coy.	
	31.		Inspected 58th and 59th Field Ambulances, 6th Wilts. R., H.Q., 58th Infy. Bde.	

WAR DIARY

of D.A.D.V.S., 19th Division.

INTELLIGENCE SUMMARY

(Erase heading not required.)

Army Form C. 2118

Instructions regarding War Diaries and Intelligence Summaries are contained in F.S. Regs., Part II. and the Staff Manual respectively. Title Pages will be prepared in manuscript.

Place	Date 1917.	Hour	Summary of Events and Information	Remarks and references to Appendices
ST JAN'S CAPPEL.	Septr 1.		Inspected 81st and 94th Field Companies and 246 M.G.Company.	
	2.		Routine work. Captain J.M.BROWN, A.V.C. left on leave.	
	3.		Inspected 56th Infantry Brigade H.Q., 7/R.Lanc.R. and M.M.P.	
	4.		Inspected Signal Company and 155 and 156 Companies, Divl. Train.	
	5.		Inspected D.H.Q. and local units.	
	6.		Inspected 8/Glouc. R. and 10/Worc. R.	
	7.		Weekly conference of Veterinary Officers at Office.	
	8.		Inspected 5/S.Wales Bord. (P) and 82nd and 94th Field Companies.	
	9.		Routine work.	
	10.		Inspected site for Clipping Depot.	
	11.		Inspected Signal Company, No. 2 Section, D.A.C. and 7/N.Lan.R. and 5/S.Wales Bord. with A.D.V.S.	
	12.		Inspected 156 and 157 Coys., Divl. Train. Moved to SCHERPENBERG.	
SCHERPEN -BURG	13.		Routine work.	
	14.		Weekly conference of Veterinary Officers at Office.	
	15.		Inspected 88th Bde., R.F.A.	
	16.		Routine work.	
	17.		Inspected 57th Infy. Bde. H.Q. and Signal Coy.	

-1-

WAR DIARY of D.A.D.V.S., 19th Division

Army Form C. 2118

D.A.D.V.S., 19th Division.

Place	Date 1917.	Hour	Summary of Events and Information	Remarks and references to Appendices
	Septr. 18.		Routine work.	
	19.		Inspected D.H.Q. and M.M.P.	
	20.		Routine work.	
	21.		Weekly conference of Veterinary Officers at Office.	
	22.		Inspected 57th and 58th Infy. Bdes. and Signal Coy. with A.D.V.S., IX Corps. Captain J.M.BROWN, A.V.C., returned from leave.	
	23.		Routine work.	
	24.		Inspected 57 M.G.Company and 9/Welsh R.	
	25.		Inspected 87 and 88 Brigades, R.F.A.	
	26.		Inspected site of Horse Clipping Dept.	
	27.		Left on leave.	

Army Form C. 2118

D.A.D.V.S.
19TH DIVISION.

No.........
Date.........

WAR DIARY
or
INTELLIGENCE SUMMARY.
(Erase heading not required.)

19th Division.

Instructions regarding War Diaries and Intelligence Summaries are contained in F. S. Regs., Part II. and the Staff Manual respectively. Title Pages will be prepared in manuscript.

Place	Date	Hour	Summary of Events and Information	Remarks and references to Appendices
ST JAN'S CAPPEL.	1917. Septr 1.		Inspected 81st and 94th Field Companies and 246 M.G.Company.	
	2.		Routine work. Captain J.M.BROWN, A.V.C. left on leave.	
	3.		Inspected 56th Infantry Brigade H.Q., 7/R.Lanc.R. and M.M.P.	
	4.		Inspected Signal Company and 155 and 156 Companies, Divl. Train.	
	5.		Inspected D.H.Q. and local units.	
	6.		Inspected 8/Glouc. R. and 10/Worc. R.	
	7.		Weekly conference of Veterinary Officers at Office.	
	8.		Inspected 5/S.Wales Bord. (P) and 82nd and 94th Field Companies.	
	9.		Routine work.	
	10.		Inspected site for Clipping Depot.	
	11.		Inspected Signal Company, No. 2 Section, D.A.C. and 7/N.Lan.R. and 5/S.Wales Bord. with A.D.V.S.	
	12.		Inspected 156 and 157 Coys., Divl. Train. Moved to SCHERPENBERG.	
SCHERPEN -BURG	13.		Routine work.	
	14.		Weekly conference of Veterinary Officers at Office.	
	15.		Inspected 88th Bde., R.F.A.	
	16.		Routine work.	
	17.		Inspected 57th Infy. Bde. H.Q. and Signal Coy.	

-1-

Army Form C. 2118

WAR DIARY
or
INTELLIGENCE SUMMARY of D.A.D.V.S., 19th Division.

Instructions regarding War Diaries and Intelligence Summaries are contained in F.S. Regs., Part II. and the Staff Manual respectively. Title Pages will be prepared in manuscript.

D.A.D.V.S.
19TH DIVISION
No ....
Date ....

Place	Date	Hour	Summary of Events and Information	Remarks and references to Appendices
	1917. Septr. 18.		Routine work.	
	19.		Inspected D.H.Q. and M.M.P.	
	20.		Routine work.	
	21.		Weekly conference of Veterinary Officers at Office.	
	22.		Inspected 57th and 58th Infy. Bdes. and Signal Coy. with A.D.V.S., IX Corps. Captain J.M.BROWN, A.V.C., returned from leave.	
	23.		Routine work.	
	24.		Inspected 57 M.G.Company and 9/Welsh R.	
	25.		Inspected 87 and 88 Brigades, R.F.A.	
	26.		Inspected site of Horse Clipping Dept.	
	27.		Left on leave.	

Jas Moore Major A.V.C.
A.D.V.S.
19th Septr 1917

D.A.D.V.S.
Army Form C. 2118
19TH DIVISION.

WAR DIARY

of

~~INTELLIGENCE SUMMARY~~

(Erase heading not required.)

Vol 2 G

Sheet I.

Instructions regarding War Diaries and Intelligence Summaries are contained in F.S. Regs., Part II. and the Staff Manual respectively. Title Pages will be prepared in manuscript.

Place	Date 1917 Oct.	Hour	Summary of Events and Information	Remarks and references to Appendices
St Jeoyer Berg.	1.		On Leave.	
	2.		"	
	3.		"	
	4.		"	
	5.		"	
	6.		"	
	7.		"	
	8.		"	
	9.		"	
	10.		Inspected Clipping Depot.	
	11.		Routine work.	
	12.		Conference of Veterinary Officers at Office.	
	13.		Routine work. Inspected 19th Signal Co.	
	14.		Inspected Clipping Depot.	
	15.		" " Inspected 27th and 22th Bdes. R.F.A.	
	16.		Inspected 27th and 22th Bdes. R.F.A.	
	17.		Routine work. Inspected 19th Signal Co.	
	18.		Inspected Horse Clipping Depot.	

WAR DIARY

Army Form C. 2118
D.A.D.V.S.
19th Division

~~INTELLIGENCE SUMMARY~~

(Erase heading not required.)

Instructions regarding War Diaries and Intelligence Summaries are contained in F.S. Regs., Part II and the Staff Manual respectively. Title Pages will be prepared in manuscript.

Sheet II.

Place	Date 1917 Oct.	Hour	Summary of Events and Information	Remarks and references to Appendices
Scherpen Berg	19.		Weekly Conference of Veterinary Officers at Office.	
	20.		Inspected Horse Clipping Depot.	
	21.		"	
	22.		Routine work.	
	23.		Inspected Horse Clipping Depot.	
	24.		Inspected 19th Signal Co. and M.M.P.	
	25.		Routine work.	
	26.		Weekly Conference of Veterinary Officers at Office.	
	27.		Inspected Horse Clipping Depot.	
	28.		"	
	29.		Inspected 87th 88th H. Bdes. R.F.A., 8 M.M.P.	
	30.		Inspected Horse Clipping Depot.	
	31.		Routine work.	

Major. A.S.C.
D.A.D.V.S. 19th Division.

Army Form C. 2118

WAR DIARY
INTELLIGENCE SUMMARY

Sheet I.

Place	Date 1917 Oct.	Hour	Summary of Events and Information	Remarks and references to Appendices
Scherpen-berg	1.		On leave.	
	2.		"	
	3.		"	
	4.		"	
	5.		"	
	6.		"	
	7.		"	
	8.		"	
	9.		"	
	10.		Inspected Horse Clipping Depot.	
	11.		Routine work.	
	12.		Conference of Veterinary Officers at Office.	
	13.		Routine work. Inspected 19th. Squad Co.	
	14.		Inspected Horse Clipping Depot.	
	15.		"	
	16.		Inspected D.H. and 00th. Bde. R.H.A.	
	17.		Routine work. Inspected 19th. Squad Co.	
	18.		Inspected Clipping Depot.	

Army Form C. 2118

WAR DIARY
INTELLIGENCE SUMMARY
(Erase heading not required.)

Instructions regarding War Diaries and Intelligence Summaries are contained in F.S. Regs., Part II. and the Staff Manual respectively. Title Pages will be prepared in manuscript.

Sheet I.

Place	Date 1917 Oct.	Hour	Summary of Events and Information	Remarks and references to Appendices
October Lefy.	19.		Weekly conference of Veterinary Officers at Office.	
	20.		Inspected Horse Clipping Depot.	
	21.		" " " "	
	22.		Routine work.	
	23.		Inspected Horse Clipping Depot.	
	24.		Inspected 9th Signal Co. & M.M.P.	
	25.		Routine work.	
	26.		Weekly conference of Veterinary Officers at Office.	
	27.		Inspected Horse Clipping Depot.	
	28.		" " " "	
	29.		Inspected 87th, 8.88th. Bdes. R.F.A. 8 M.M.P.	
	30.		Inspected Horse Clipping Depot.	
	31.		Routine work.	

Major. A.V.C.
A.D.V.S.; 19th Division.

Army Form C. 2118

WAR DIARY

~~INTELLIGENCE SUMMARY~~

(Erase heading not required.)

Sheet 1.

Instructions regarding War Diaries and Intelligence Summaries are contained in F.S. Regs., Part II. and the Staff Manual respectively. Title Pages will be prepared in manuscript.

Place	Date	Hour	Summary of Events and Information	Remarks and references to Appendices
Steenbecque	1914 Nov. 1.		Inspected 19th Division Central Horse Clipping Depot.	
	2.		Weekly conference of Veterinary Officers at Office.	
	3.		Inspected 19th Division Central Horse Clipping Depot.	
	4.		" 19th Division Signal Co.	
	5.		" 2nd Machine Gun Coy. — 5th South Wales Borderers — 19th Division Central Horse Clipping Depot.	
	6.		" "	
	7.		" "	
	8.		" 57th Field Ambulance.	
	9.		" 19th Signal Co. & 19th Division Central Horse Clipping Depot.	
	10.		Weekly conference of Veterinary Officers at Office.	
St. Jans Capel	11.		Moved to.	
	12.		Routine work.	
Blaringhem	13.		Moved to.	
	14.		Inspected H.Q. 57th Infantry Brigade.	
	15.		" of Flanders & 9th Royal West Fusiliers — 8 & 7th Field Ambulance.	
	16.		Routine work.	
	17.		Weekly conference of Veterinary Officers at Office. Inspected 8/9th Field Coy. R.E.	
	18.		Routine work. Inspected J.H.D. Signal Coy.	
	19.		" " Signal Coy.	
	20.		Inspected Signal Coy 8 & 7th Machine Gun Coy.	

Army Form C. 2118

WAR DIARY
~~INTELLIGENCE SUMMARY~~
(Erase heading not required.)

Sheet W.

Place	Date	Hour	Summary of Events and Information	Remarks and references to Appendices
Blaringhem	20.		Inspected 7th East Lancs — 7th Kings Own Royal Lancs — 7th South Lancs — 8 56th Machine Gun Coy.	
	21.		Routine work.	
	22.		To Corps H.Q. acting A.A. & S.S., IX Corps.	
	23.		Inspected 19th Division Central Horse Clipping Depot.	
	24.		" 8th Brigade R.F.A.	
	25.		IX Corps H.Q. & 8 Horse trip.	
	26.		Conference with A.A. & S.S. 2nd Army at IX Corps.	
	27.		Inspected 2/88th Brigade R.F.A. & 154 Coy. A.S.C.	
	28.		" 19th Division Central Horse Clipping Depot.	
	29.		" 15th Reserve Park.	
	30.		" 152 Btty. R. Artillery.	

Sgd. Major. A.V.C.
A.D.V.S., 19th Division.

WAR DIARY
~~INTELLIGENCE SUMMARY~~

(Erase heading not required.)

Army Form C. 2118

Instructions regarding War Diaries and Intelligence Summaries are contained in F.S. Regs., Part II. and the Staff Manual respectively. Title Pages will be prepared in manuscript.

Place	Date 1917	Hour	Summary of Events and Information	Remarks and references to Appendices
Scherpenberg	Nov. 1.		Inspected 19th Division Central Horse Clipping Depot.	
	2.		Weekly conference of Veterinary Officers at Office.	
	3.		Inspected 19th Division Central Horse Clipping Depot.	
	4.		" 19th Division Signal Co.	
	5.		" 2nd Machine Gun Coy. — 5/ South Wales Borderers — 19th.	
	6.		" Division Central Horse Clipping Depot.	
	7.		" 19th Division " " " "	
	8.		" 57th Field Ambulance.	
	9.		" Signal Co. & 19th Division Central Horse Clipping Depot.	
	10.		Weekly conference of Veterinary Officers at Office.	
St Jans Capel	11.		Moved to. Inspected 19th Division Central Horse Clipping Depot.	
Blaringhem	12.		Routine work. " " "	
	13.		Moved to.	
	14.		Inspected M.A. 57th Infantry Brigade.	
	15.		" Squadron 9th Royal Welsh Fusiliers & 57th Field Ambulance.	
	16.		Routine work.	
	17.		Weekly conference of Veterinary Officers at Office. Inspected 21st Field Coy. R.E.	
	18.		Routine work. Inspected L.H.A. animals. Signal Coy.	
	19.		Inspected Signal Coy. & 57th Machine Gun Coy.	

Army Form C. 2118

WAR DIARY
INTELLIGENCE SUMMARY
(Erase heading not required.)

Sheet 11

Place	Date	Hour	Summary of Events and Information	Remarks and references to Appendices
Blaringhem	1917 Nov 20		Inspected 7th East Lancs ~ 7th Kings Own Royal Lancs ~ 7th South Lancs & 56th Machine Gun Coy.	
	21.		Routine work.	
	22.		To Corps H.Q., acting A.D.S.S., IX Corps.	
	23.		Inspected 19th Division Central Horse Clipping Depot.	
	24.		" 87th Bde. P.H.Q.	
	25.		" IX Corps M.T.S. & Horse Sick.	
	26.		Conference with A.D.S.S, 2nd Army at IX Corps.	
	27.		Inspected Q/88th Bde. P.H.Q. 8 15th Coy A.S.C.	
	28.		" 19th Division Central Horse Clipping Depot.	
	29.		" 15th Reserve Park.	
	30.		" 152 Bty, R.A.	

Major A.V.C.
A.A.D.S.S. 19th Division

WAR DIARY

Army Form C. 2118

Instructions regarding War Diaries and Intelligence Summaries are contained in F.S. Regs., Part II. and the Staff Manual respectively. Title Pages will be prepared in manuscript.

(Erase heading not required.)

Sheet 1.

Place	Date	Hour	Summary of Events and Information	Remarks and references to Appendices
	1917 Decembr			
Blaringhem	1.		Inspected 37th Division Central Horse Clipping Depot and 5th South Wales Borderers.	
	2.		Inspected 19th Division Central Horse Clipping Depot, IX Corps Horse Hosp. No. 8 & IX Corps Mobile Veterinary Detachment.	
	3.		Inspected 149th Bde. R.F.A., 30th Division.	
	4.		" " 30th Division Central Horse Clipping Depot.	
	5.		Left IX Corps for Blaringhem.	
	6.		Weekly conference of Veterinary Officers at office.	
	7.		Moved to Bavelos.	
	8.		" Acquet-le-Petit.	
	9.		" Ericourt.	
	10.		Inspected 236th Bde. R.F.A. 47th Division for Remarks.	
	11.		" Routine wk. P.	
	12.		"	
	13.		Weekly conference of Veterinary Officers at office.	
Henneville Bourjonval	14.		Lived to Henneville Bourjonval.	
	15.		Inspected 57th Inf Bde. & found 1 case Ichinakits in 4th Bedfords, 6 3rd R.M.S.	
	16.		Inspected 19th Squad Co.	

Army Form C. 2118

WAR DIARY
~~INTELLIGENCE~~ SUMMARY
(Erase heading not required.)

Instructions regarding War Diaries and Intelligence Summaries are contained in F.S. Regs., Part II. and the Staff Manual respectively. Title Pages will be prepared in manuscript.

Sheet 2.

Place	Date	Hour	Summary of Events and Information	Remarks and references to Appendices
Neuville Bourjonval	1917 December 17.		Inspected 82nd J. Co. R.E.	
	18.		57th Infy. Bde. & 19th Signal Co.	
	19.		S.H.D., M.O., R.A. & M.T.	
	20.		Routine work.	
	21.		Weekly conference of Veterinary Officers at Office.	
	22.		Routine work.	
	23.		Inspected L.H.A. animals.	
	24.		" 56th & 58th Infantry Brigades.	
	25.		" 19th Signal Co.	
	26.		" 81/84 M.V.S.	
	27.		" 19th Signal Co.	
	28.		Weekly conference of Veterinary Officers at Office.	
	29.		Routine work.	
	30.		Inspected 19th Signal Co.	
	31.		" 57th Infty. Bde.	

Ja——
Major. A.V.C.
A.D.V.S. 19th Division.

WAR DIARY
INTELLIGENCE SUMMARY

Army Form C. 2118

War Diary VIII 92

Sheet 23.

Place	Date Hour	Summary of Events and Information	Remarks and references to Appendices
Blaringhem	1917 September 1.	Inspected 37th Division Central Horse Clipping Depot & 5th South Wales Borderers.	
	2.	Inspected 19th Division Central Horse Clipping Depot & Corps Horse Hosp & IX Corps Mobile Vety Detachment.	
	3.	Inspected 149th Bde. R.F.A. 30th Division.	
	4.	" 30th Division Central Horse Clipping Depot.	
	5.	Left IV Corps for Blaringhem.	
	6.	Weekly conference of Veterinary Officers at Office.	
	7.	Moved to Bavinchove.	
	8.	" Acheit-le-Petit.	
	9.	" Etricourt.	
	10.		
	11.	Inspected 236th Bde. R.F.A. 47th Division. Routine work.	
	12.	"	
	13.		
	14.	Weekly conference of Veterinary Officers at Office.	
Neuville Bourjonval	15.	Inspected 57th Inf. Bde. Found horse lines Bourjonval in f.s. Bedfords 63rd Bde. R.W.D.	

Army Form C. 2118

WAR DIARY
INTELLIGENCE SUMMARY
(Erase heading not required.)

Instructions regarding War Diaries and Intelligence Summaries are contained in F.S. Regs., Part II. and the Staff Manual respectively. Title Pages will be prepared in manuscript.

Place	Date	Hour	Summary of Events and Information	Remarks and references to Appendices
Meuvelle Bourjonval	1917 December 16		Inspected 19th Squad Co.	See A.I.
	17.		" 82nd Fy. L Co. R.E.	
	18.		" 57th Infty. Bde. 8 & 19th Squad Co.	
	19.		" J.H.D. H.Q., C.A.S.M.C.	
	20.		Routine work.	
	21.		Weekly conference of Veterinary Officers at Office.	
	22.		Routine work.	
	23.		Inspected J.H.D.	
	24.		" 56th & 58th Infantry Brigades.	
	25.		" 19th Squad Co.	
	26.		" 51st M.T.S.	
	27.		" 19th Squad Co.	
	28.		Weekly conference of Veterinary Officers at Office.	
	29.		Routine work.	
	30.		Inspected 19th Squad Co.	
	31.		" 57th Infantry Bde.	

Hassell Major, A.D.C.
A.D.V.S. 19th Division

Army Form C. 2118

WAR DIARY
INTELLIGENCE SUMMARY
(Erase heading not required.)

Instructions regarding War Diaries and Intelligence Summaries are contained in F. S. Regs., Part II. and the Staff Manual respectively. Title Pages will be prepared in manuscript.

Sheet 1.

Place	Date	Hour	Summary of Events and Information	Remarks and references to Appendices
Neuville Bourjonval	1918 January 1.		Routine work R.	
	2.		Inspected 82nd F. Coy. R.E.	
	3.		Weekly conference of Veterinary Officers at Office.	
	4.		Routine work R.	
	5.		Inspected 84th & 88th Bdes. R.F.A.	
	6.		" 135 F. Heavy Bty. R.G.A.	
	7.		" Signals & F.H.A.	
	8.		" 5 F. Infantry Brigade.	
	9.		Routine work R.	
	10.		Inspected 290 F. A.L. Bde. Weekly conference of Veterinary Officers at Office.	
	11.		" 8 Glosters. Matterined 13/290 F. A.L. Bde.	
	12.		" 290 F. A.L. Bde.	
	13.		"	
	14.		"	
	15.		"	
	16.		" N.C. Lancs. — 84 F. & 88 F. Bde. R.F.A.	
	17.		" 80 F. & 59 F. Field Ambulances — 82nd F. Co. R.E. — 5/R.W.B.	
	18.		" 84 F. & 94 F. F. Cos. R.E. Weekly conference at Office.	
	19.		Divisional Train & M.M.P.	
			Called on A.D.V.S. at Corps.	

Army Form C. 2118

WAR DIARY
~~INTELLIGENCE SUMMARY~~
(Erase heading not required.)

Instructions regarding War Diaries and Intelligence Summaries are contained in F. S. Regs., Part II. and the Staff Manual respectively. Title Pages will be prepared in manuscript.

Sheet II.

Place	Date 1918 January	Hour	Summary of Events and Information	Remarks and references to Appendices
Neuville Bourjonval	20.		Inspected 54th & 58th Infantry Bdes. — 246th M. L. Co. — 404th Bde. R.F.A.	
	21.		Called on A.D.V.S. at Corps.	
	22.		Inspected 4th M. Laws — 4th L Laws in Linato.	
	23.		" 21st & 94th L Cos. R.E. — 58th L Laws.	
	24.		" 82nd L Co. R.E. — 84th & 220th Bdes. R.F.A. — 4th Kingsmen — 4th L Laws. Conference at Office.	
	25.		" Linato — 15th Coy. A.E.C. — 5/5. W.B.	
	26.		Routine work.	
	27.		Inspected 154 Coy. A.S.C. — 56th Supply Bde. — Linato.	
	28.		" 54th Supply Bde. — 54th M.L. Coy.	
	29.		" 81st & 94th Lieut R.E. — 5/5. W.B.	
	30.		" remounts for F.A. & sent 1 with Inspected Maupe to 31 M.V.S. — 58th Infantry Bde. — 246th M.L. Coy.	
	31.		" F.A. remounts & sent 3 to 31 M.V.S. for scrapings & examination for Mange.	

J.G.S.
Major. A. V.C.
A. D. V. S. 19th Division.

WAR DIARY

INTELLIGENCE SUMMARY

Army Form C 2118

Sheet 1.

Place	Date 1918 January	Hour	Summary of Events and Information	Remarks and references to Appendices
Neuville Bourjonval	1.		Routine work.	
	2.		Inspected 82nd L. Co. R.E.	
	3.		Weekly conference at Office.	
	4.		Routine work.	
	5.		Inspected 94th & 88th Bdes. R.F.A.	
	6.		" 135th H. Bty. R.F.A.	
	7.		" Divnl. S.A.H.Q.	
	8.		" 54th Infantry Bde.	
	9.		Routine work.	
	10.		Inspected 298th A.T. Bde. Weekly conference at Office.	
	11.		" Flockes. Mallerie B/298 F. 2 A.T. Bde.	
	12.		" 298 F. A.T. Bde.	
	13.		" " "	
	14.		" " "	
	15.		" " "	
	16.		" 57 F. & 59 F. F. Ambulances — 94th & 88th Bdes. R.F.A.	
	17.		" 81st & 94th F. Cos. R.E. Weekly conference at Office.	
	18.		" Divisional Train & M.M.P.	
	19.		Called on A.D.M.S. at Corps.	

Army Form C. 2118

WAR DIARY
INTELLIGENCE SUMMARY

(Erase heading not required.)

Sheet II

Place	Date	Hour	Summary of Events and Information	Remarks and references to Appendices
Feuville Bourgonval	1918 January 20.		Inspected 57th & 58th Infantry Brigades. — 246th M.G. Co. — 178/4 Bde. R.F.A.	
	21.		Called on A.D.V.S. at Corps.	
	22.		Inspected 11th Lancs. 8 Yth. L. Lancs. Signal Co.	
	23.		" 21st & 89th L. Co. R.E. 8 58th & 59th L. Ambulances.	
	24.		" 82nd L. Co. R.E. — 24th & 88th Bdes. R.F.A. — 4th Kings Own — 4th L. Lancs. Conference at Office.	
	25.		" Signal Co. — 154 Coy. A.S.C. — 5/2. W.R.	
	26.		Routine work.	
	27.		Inspected 154 Coy. A.S.C. — 56th Suffy. Bde. — Signals.	
	28.		" 54th Suffy. Bde. — 54th M.G. Co.	
	29.		" 21st & 89th L.Co. R.E. — 5/2. W.R.	
	30.		" remounts for R.A. Sent 1 with Inspected Mange to 31 M.V.S. Infantry Bde. — 246 M.G. Coy.	
	31.		" R.A. remounts sent 3 to 31 M.V.S. for scraping's & examination for Mange.	

Wilson
Lieut.
Major. A.V.C.
A.D.V.S. Gd 19th Division.

WAR DIARY

~~INTELLIGENCE SUMMARY~~

Army Form C. 2118

PART I-8 19D

Place	Date 1918	Hour	Summary of Events and Information	Remarks and references to Appendices
Merville Rougeoul	Feby 1st		Inspected Signals in Called on A.D.M.S. at 5th Corps.	
	2.		" Remands for Advisory in Inspected 15th Co. R.A.C. & detected two cases as suspicious skin disease.	
	3.		Proceeded to Bethencourt & inspected 1 dane of 19th A.C. isolated as a suspicious case of Epizootic Lymphangitis.	
	4.		Inspected 56th Infantry Brigade.	
	5.		F.M.O. on M.M.P. in Picardie ward.	
	6.		Re-examined dane of F.A.C. isolated as a suspicious case of Epizootic Lymphangitis. Left on leave for England.	
	7.		On leave.	
	8.		"	
	9.		"	
	10.		"	
	11.		"	
	12.		"	
	13.		"	

Army Form C. 2118

WAR DIARY

~~INTELLIGENCE SUMMARY~~

(Erase heading not required.)

Instructions regarding War Diaries and Intelligence Summaries are contained in F. S. Regs., Part II. and the Staff Manual respectively. Title Pages will be prepared in manuscript.

Place	Date	Hour	Summary of Events and Information	Remarks and references to Appendices
	1918 Feb.			
	14.		On leave.	
	15.		"	
	16.		"	
	17.		"	
	18.		"	
	19.		"	
	20.		"	
	21.		Returned to France from leave to England.	
	22.		Travelling.	
Haplincourt	23.		Arrived at Divisional Headquarters.	
	24.		Inspected Artillery remounts.	
	25.		" " " 3/4 M.T.S. - equines.	
	26.		" " " 56 H. - 57 H. - 58 H. & 240 M.G. Coy.	
	27.		" " " Helped to classify animals.	
	28.		Conference of Veterinary officers at office.	"

Hoslyn Major A.V.C.
A.D.V.S. 19th Division

WAR DIARY
INTELLIGENCE SUMMARY

Place	Date	Hour	Summary of Events and Information	Remarks and references to Appendices
Neuville Bourjonval	Feby 1918 1st		Inspected Signals – Called in A.D.V.S. at 5th Corps.	
	2.		" Inspected 15th Coy. A.S.C. Remounts for the Artillery – Inspected this I/case.	
	3.		Selected two cases as suspicious skin I/case. Proceeded to Bertincourt & inspected Horse of 192 M.A.C. isolated as a suspicious case of Epizootic Lymphangitis.	
	4.		Inspected 56th Infantry Brigade.	
	5.		" H.Q. – M.M.P. – Routine work.	
	6.		Received Horse of M.A.C. isolated as a suspicious case of Epizootic Lymphangitis. Left on leave for England.	
	7.		On leave.	
	8.		"	
	9.		"	
	10.		"	
	11.		"	
	12.		"	
	13.		"	

Army Form C. 2118

WAR DIARY of INTELLIGENCE SUMMARY

(Erase heading not required.)

Instructions regarding War Diaries and Intelligence Summaries are contained in F. S. Regs., Part II. and the Staff Manual respectively. Title Pages will be prepared in manuscript.

Place	Date	Hour	Summary of Events and Information	Remarks and references to Appendices
	Feb.			
	14.		On Leave.	
	15.		"	
	16.		"	
	17.		"	
	18.		"	
	19.		"	
	20.		"	
	21.		Returned to France from leave to England.	
	22.		Travelling.	
	23.		Arrived at Divisional Headquarters.	
Hopoutre	24.		Inspected Artillery remounts	
	25.		" 31st M.T.C.	
	26.		" 56th, 57th, 58th & 24th M.Gun Coys.	
	27.		" " " & helped to classify animals	
	28.		Conference of D.A.Ds. at Officers " "	

Lascure(?)
Major. A.D.C.
H.Q.V.S., 19th Division.

WAR DIARY

INTELLIGENCE SUMMARY

Army Form C. 2118

Place	Date 1918	Hour	Summary of Events and Information	Remarks and references to Appendices
Neuville Bourjonval	Feby 1st		Inspected Signals — Called on A.H.V.S. at 5th Corps.	
	2.		" Remounts for the Artillery — Inspected 15th Coy. A.S.C. & detected two cases as suspicious Skin Disease.	
	3.		Proceeded to Bertincourt & inspected 1 horse of 19th H.A.C. isolated as a suspicious case of Epizootic Lymphangitis.	
	4.		Inspected 56th Infantry Brigade.	
	5.		" V.H.Q. — M.M.P. — Routine work.	
	6.		Received Horse of H.A.C. isolated as a suspicious case of Epizootic Lymphangitis. Left on leave for England.	
	7.		On leave.	
	8.		"	
	9.		"	
	10.		"	
	11.		"	
	12.		"	
	13.		"	

Army Form C. 2118

WAR DIARY
INTELLIGENCE SUMMARY
(Erase heading not required.)

Instructions regarding War Diaries and Intelligence Summaries are contained in F. S. Regs., Part II. and the Staff Manual respectively. Title Pages will be prepared in manuscript.

Place	Date 1917 Feb	Hour	Summary of Events and Information	Remarks and references to Appendices
	14.		On leave.	
	15.		"	
	16.		"	
	17.		"	
	18.		"	
	19.		"	
	20.		"	
	21.		Returned to France from leave to England.	
	22.		Travelling.	
Staplincourt	23.		Arrived at Divisional Headquarters.	
	24.		Inspected artillery remounts.	
	25.		" 314 M.T.S. in Signals.	
	26.		" 56th – 57th 58th & 346th M.G. Coy.	
	27.		" " " & helped to classify animals	
	28.		Conference of Veterinary Officers at Office. " "	

Signed Major A.V.C.
A.D.V.S., 19th Division.

WAR DIARY

INTELLIGENCE SUMMARY

(Erase heading not required.)

Army Form C. 2118.

of Major L.A.S. Moore. A.D. Army S., H.Q.D.S., 19th Division.

Place	Date	Hour	Summary of Events and Information	Remarks and references to Appendices
Hapilmcourt	1918 March 1.		Inspected 4th South Lancs — 4th E. Lancs — 4th Kings Own & Recruits for R.A. Signal Coy. 8 L. 58. F. A.	Sheet 1. VR 3
	2.		Routine work.	
	3.		Inspected 58th Field Ambulance — 58th Suffly. Bde. H.Q. & transport of Units. 9th. 8.82nd L. Coy. R.E. — 6/S.W.B.	
	4.		" 5th Suffly. Bde. Transport & Hiund. M. Gun Bttn.	
	5.		" 3rd M.T.S. at Le Mesnil.	
	6.		" 10th Worcesters — 4th S. Lancs — 4th Kings Own — 167 Coy. A.S.C.	
	7.		" Signal Coy & M.M.P. Conference of D.O.s. at Office.	
	8.		" 58th L. Ambulance 8 58th Suffly Bde H.Q. 8 Units.	
	9.		" 57th L. Ambulance — 81st L. Coy. R.E.	
	10.		Routine work.	
	11.		Inspected 4th E. Lancs — 4th Kings Own — 9th Cheshires 8.89th Trustees.	
	12.		" Hind M. Gun Bttn. — A.H.D.S., 5th Corps called.	
	13.		" 81st 8.80th Bdes. R.F.A.	
	14.		" M.M.P. Signato — M.H.A. — Conference of D.O.s. at Office.	
	15.		" 58th Suffly Bdes. — 82nd. 89th L. Coy. R.E.	
	16.		Attended conference at office of H.T.S. 3rd Army.	
	17.		Routine work — Inspected signal Coy.	
	18.		Inspected 9th Cheshires Hind. M. Gun Bttn 1/4th Shropshire L. Infy.	
	19.		" H.H.R. 8 M.M.P.	

Army Form C. 2118.

WAR DIARY
or
INTELLIGENCE SUMMARY.
(Erase heading not required.)

Instructions regarding War Diaries and Intelligence Summaries are contained in F. S. Regs., Part II. and the Staff Manual respectively. Title pages will be prepared in manuscript.

Sheet I.

Place	Date 1918 March	Hour	Summary of Events and Information	Remarks and references to Appendices
Haplincourt	20.		Routine work.	
	21.		Inspected Signal Coy. — Conference of S.O's at Office.	
	22.		Moved to Bancourt.	
	23.		" Grevillers. M.D.S. moved to Le Transloy — inspd. 10th Warwicks.	
	24.		" Achiet le Petit — Moved to Puisieux.	
	25.		" Puisieux, Colincamps then to Fonquevillers.	
	26.		" Fonvier and then to La Cauchie. Inspected 58th Suffk. Rde.	
	27.		Inspected Hinnl. M. Guy Batty. in 57th Inf. Bde. — 5/5. W.B.	
	28.		Conference of S.O's at Office. — M.D.S. evacuated 21 arrivals by rail.	
	29.		Left La Cauchie for entraining at Houdains for 2nd Army — arrived Gravouthe	
	30.		A.D.M.S. Australian Corps called — inspected Signal Coy & H.Q. H.A.	
Gravouthe	31.		3/4. M.D.S. arrived at Gravouthe.	

Lt Major A.D.C.
D.A.D.M.S. 19th Division.

Duplicate

WAR DIARY of Major L.A.S. Moore. A.S.C., Army Form C. 2118.
~~INTELLIGENCE SUMMARY~~ H.Q. L. of C., 19th Division

Instructions regarding War Diaries and Intelligence Summaries are contained in F.S. Regs., Part II. and the Staff Manual respectively. Title pages will be prepared in manuscript.

Sheet 1

(Erase heading not required.)

Place	Date	Hour	Summary of Events and Information	Remarks and references to Appendices
Staplecourt	1918 March 1		Inspected 4th South Lancs — 4/4th E. Lancs — 1/4th Kings Own & Remounts for P.Q. & L.S.O.	
	2.		Visited 8 H.S.O.	
	3.		Routine work.	
	4.		Inspected 58th F. Ambulance — 58th F. Supply Bde. H.Q. & transport of units. 94th, 88nd, 82nd L. Cos. R.E. — 5/S. W.B.	
	5.		" 57th Infantry Bde. Transport & Mmt. M. Gun Bttn.	
	6.		" 3/oy M.D.S. at Le Meurie	
	7.		" 10th Worcesters — 1/4th S. Lancs. — 1/4th Kings Own — 157 Coy. A.S.C. Signal Coy 4th M.M.P. — Conference of M.O.s at Office.	
	8.		" 58th L. Ambulance & 58th F. Supply Bde. H.Q. & transport	
	9.		" 57th L. Ambulance — 81st L. Troy. F.E.	
	10.		Routine work.	
	11.		Inspected 4th E. Lancs — 4th S. Lancs — 1/4th Kings Own — 9th F. Creatives & 8th Glosters.	
	12.		" Mmt. M. Gun Bttn — O.H.S.Q. 5th Corps called	
	13.		" 84th & 88th Bde. R.L.A.	
	14.		" M.M.P. Signals	
	15.		" Mmt. M. Gun Bttn — L.M.A. — conference of M.O.s at Office.	
	16.		" 58th L. Supply Bde. — 82 coy. & 94th L. Cos. R.E.	
	17.		Attended conference at Office of L.L. of C., 3rd Army.	
	18.		Routine work — Inspected Signal Coy.	
	19.		Inspected 9th F. Creatives — Mmt. M. Gun Bttn — 1/4th Loyshire L. Supply. H.L.A. & M.M.P.	

Army Form C. 2118.

WAR DIARY
or
INTELLIGENCE SUMMARY.
(Erase heading not required.)

Sheet 2

Place	Date 1918 March	Hour	Summary of Events and Information	Remarks and references to Appendices
Haplincourt	20.		Routine work.	
	21.		Inspected Signal Coy. – Conference of Sen. Officers at Office.	
	22.		Moved to Barrcourt.	
	23.		Lewis gun 3½ M.T.S. moved to Le Transloy – night 10th Warwicks.	
	24.		" Active Le Petit M.T.S. moved to Burgroy.	
	25.		" Review, Colincamps & then to Longueviller.	
	26.		" Parouier and then to Ja Cautie. Inspected 58th Inf. Bde.	
	27.		Inspected Hime M. Gun Btty. – 57th Inf. Bde. – 5/57 M.T.S.	
	28.		Conference of Sen. Officers at Office – M.T.S. evacuated 21 animals by rail.	
	29.		Left La Cautie for remaining H.T. Horses for 2nd Army – arrived Havanhe.	
Havanhe	30.		A.D.V.S. Australian Corps called. – Inspected Signal Coy H.H.A.C.	
	31.		3¼ M.T.S. arrived at Havanhe.	

Date of formation } of Division } September 1914.

Date of formation } of 3¼ M.T.S. } 18-4-15.

Date of proceeding } H.Q. 17-7-15.
overseas } M.T.S. 19-7-15.

Assistant Major. A.D.C.
H.A.D.S. 19th Division.

Army Form C. 2118.

WAR DIARY
INTELLIGENCE SUMMARY of Major J.A.S. Moore. A.L.

(Erase heading not required.)

Sheet 1.

Place	Date	Hour	Summary of Events and Information	Remarks and references to Appendices
Granache.	Apl. 1.		Called on H.Q. 1st, 2nd Australian Division and made arrangements to take over site of 2nd Australian M.T.S. at B.P.O. S.B. Sheet 3G.	
	2.		Moved to Stove Camp. Inspected Machine Gun Battalion — 9th West 89th Royal Welsh Fus transport. Inspected site to be taken over by 2nd M.T.S. of B.P.O. S.B.	
	3.		Called on H.Q. 1st & 2nd Australian Division and took over Range Service. Inspected Machine Gun Battalion and 58th Infantry Brigade transport.	
	4.		Attended conference at office of A.D.T. Australian Corps.	
	5.		Inspected 87th Bde. R.F.A. animals embarked on Barge at Bac St Maur.	
	6.		Routine work.	
	7.		Inspected H.A.C. & Signal Coy. animals.	
	8.		H.A.C. less 40 animals & 2 section out grazing.	
	9.		Attended at Bac St Maur to see animals embarked on Barge when embarkation not carried out owing to Barge Selective.	
	10.		Inspected transport of 21st, 92nd Bdg. & 94th 2. Coy. R.E. & 5th South Wales Borderers. Moved to Granache.	
Granache.	11.		Moved to Mont Moir. Inspected transport of 57th Infantry Bde. – Machine Gun Battalion – 15th Coy. A.C.C. & 2nd M.S.O.	
Mont Moir.	12.		Inspected remounts arrived at 15th Coy. A.S.C. lines – M.M.F. animals with A.P.M. – 2nd M.T.S. moved to Reuctepe.	
	13.		Moved to Westoutre. – 2nd M.T.S. moved to Wippenhoek.	
Westoutre.	14.		Inspected transport of 56th, 57th, & 58th, & 58th Infantry Brigades – 81st, 82nd, 89th & Coy. R.E. & 5th South Wales Borderers.	
	15.		Inspected A.E. & C. Batteries 88th Bde. R.F.A. – A.S.C. Batteries 87th Bde. R.F.A. & 19th Signal Company.	
	16.		Col. Colonel Montgomery's horse which was suffering from chest wound, also horse of 19th Signal Coy. for chest wounds.	
	17.		Moved to Abeele Aerodrome. 2/17 M.T.S. moved to Abeele aerodrome. Called on A.D.T.S. 9th Corps.	

D.D. & L., London, E.C. Sch B2 Forms/C2118/14
(A8001) Wt. W.1771/M2031 750,000 5/17

Army Form C. 2118.

WAR DIARY

of ~~INTELLIGENCE SUMMARY~~

(Erase heading not required.)

Major. L.A.S. Moore. A.V.C.

Sheet II

Place	Date 1918 April	Hour	Summary of Events and Information	Remarks and references to Appendices
Obeele (Aerodrome)	18.		Conference with H.Q.V.S., 83rd Division. Conference of Veterinary Officers at Office. Inspected transport of 56th, 67th, & 58th Infantry Brigades - 81st & 2nd 89th R.E. & South Wales Borderers animals of 58th Wales Borderers beginning to loop hair.	
	19.		Routine work.	
	20.			
	21.		Moved to Proven. 31st M.V.S. moved to Proven.	
Proven	22.		Inspected animals of M.M.P. & 19th Signal Company	
	23.		31st M.V.S. moved to Stadenvelde by order of A.D.V.S. 9th Corps to receive animals from French Army. Inspected transport of Machine Gun Battalion.	
	24.		Inspected 31st M.V.S. at Stadenvelde.	
	25.		Inspected transport of Glosters - 10th Warwicks - 59th F. Ambulance - S/South Wales Borders - 82nd & 94th L. Cos. R.E. & 56th Infantry Brigade. Conference of Veterinary Officers at office.	
	26.		Inspected C/87 Bde. R.L.A. 8 sent in to 31st M.V.S. suffering from Debility & 4 suffering from Debility in C/87 Bde. R.L.A.	
	27.		Inspected the foregoing units & sent in animals suffering from Debility to 31st M.V.S. D/87 Bde. R.L.A. 5 — A/87 Bde. R.L.A. 1 — C/87 Bde. R.L.A. 7 — & B/87 Bde. R.L.A. 5.	
	28.		Inspected animals of H.Q.A. & M.M.P.	
	29.		Moved to L.18. Central. Sheet 27. Inspected 58th F. Ambulance & Divisional Train.	
L.13 Central (Sheet 27)	30.		Routine work. Inspected 31st M.V.S.	

Joshua
Major. A.V.C.
A.D.V.S., 19th Division.

Duplicate

WAR DIARY

Army Form C. 2118.

Instructions regarding War Diaries and Intelligence Summaries are contained in F.S. Regs., Part II. and the Staff Manual respectively. Title pages will be prepared in manuscript.

INTELLIGENCE SUMMARY of ~~~~~~~~~~~ Major in Charge of Horses. A.I.C.

(Erase heading not required.)

Place	Date 1918 April	Hour	Summary of Events and Information	Remarks and references to Appendices
			Sheet I	
Franvillers	1.		Called on D.A.D.V.S. 2nd Australian Division and made arrangements to take over site of 2nd Australian M.T.S. at B.S.O. & V.S. Sheet 36.	
	2.		Moved to Horse Camp. Inspected Machine Gun Battalion - 9th West & 9th Royal Welsh Fus. transport. Inspected site to be taken over by 3/9th M.T.S. at B.S.O. & V.S.	
Horse Camp	3.		Called on D.A.D.V.S. 2nd Australian Division and took over Horse service. Inspected Machine Gun Batt. & 58th Infantry Bde. transport.	
	4.		Attended conference at office of A.D.V.S. Australian Corps.	
	5.		Inspected 27th Bde. R.F.A. Convalescents embarked to Rouge at Bac St Maur.	
	6.		Routine work.	
	7.		Inspected V.A.P. & Signal Coy. animals.	
	8.		V.A.C. less 40 animals of 2 Section out grazing.	
	9.		Attended at Bac St Maur to see animals embarked on barge when an alteration was caused ... dying to heavy shelling.	
	10.		Inspected transport of 91st, 82nd, 89th Div. R.E. & of South Wales Borderers. Moved to Franroure.	
Franroure	11.		Moved to Mont Noir. Inspected transport of 57th Infantry Bde. — Machine Gun Battalion — 10th Cav. A.C. & 3/9th M.T.S.	
Mont Noir	12.		Inspected remounts arrived at 15th Cav. A.D.C. lines — M.M.P. animals with D.A.M. — 3/9th M.T.S. moved to Boeschepe.	
	13.		Moved to Westoutre. Inspected 3/9th M.T.S. moved to Zippendet.	
Westoutre	14.		Inspected transport of 56th, 67th & 58th Infantry Brigades — 9th, 72nd & 94th Div. R.E. & of South Wales Borderers.	
	15.		Inspected A.B. & C. Batteries 22nd Bde. R.F.A. — A.B.C. Batteries 27th Bde. R.F.A. & V.A.P. & Signal Coy.	
	16.		Lt Colonel Montgomery horse which was suffering from shell wound, also horse of 19th Signal Coy for shell wound.	
	17.		Moved to Abeele. 3/9th M.T.S. moved to Abeele aerodrome. Called on A.D.V.S. 9th Corps.	

Duplicate

Army Form C. 2118.

WAR DIARY

~~INTELLIGENCE SUMMARY~~ of Major A.D.S. Moore. A.D.V.S.

(Erase heading not required.)

Instructions regarding War Diaries and Intelligence Summaries are contained in F.S. Regs., Part II. and the Staff Manual respectively. Title pages will be prepared in manuscript.

Sheet II

Place	Date April	Hour	Summary of Events and Information	Remarks and references to Appendices
Steele (Previous)	18.		Conference with H.Q. V.S. 33rd Division. Conference of Veterinary Officers at Office. Inspected transport of 56th, 57th & 58th Infantry Brigades.— 81st, 82nd & 94th F.Co. R.E. & S/park.	
	19.		Visited Borderers. animals of 57th. W. B. beginning to look thin.	
	20.		Routine work.	
	21.		Moved to Proven. 33rd M.V.S. moved to Proven.	
Proven.	22.		Inspected animals of M.M.P. & 19th. Signal Coy.	
	23.		33rd M.V.S. moved to Oedeweroevelde by order of A.D.M.S. 9th. Corps to receive animals from sick duty. Inspected transport of Machine Gun Battalion.	
	24.		Inspected 33rd M.V.S. at Oedeweroevelde	
	25.		Inspected transport of 8/Yorkers — 10/Warwicks — 59th L. Ambulance — 1/South Wales Borderers— 82nd & 94th F.Co. R.E.— 8 & 56th. Infantry Bde. Conference of Veterinary Officers at office.	
	26.		Inspected 9/87 Bde. R.S.a. 8 sent in 2 horses to 33rd M.V.S. suffering from Debility 8 + suffering from Debility in 2/88 Bde. R.S.a.	
	27.		Inspected the following units & sent in animals suffering from Debility to 33rd M.V.S. 4/87 Bde. R.S.a. 5 — 9/87 Bde. R.S.a. 1 — 9/87 Bde. R.S.a. 7 & 9/88 Bde. R.S.a. 5.	
	28.		Inspected animals of H.Q. & M.M.P.	
	29.		Moved to L. 13. central. Sheet 27. Inspected 52th. L. Ambulance Divisional Train	
L.13.central (Sheet 27.)	30.		Routine work. Inspected 33rd M.V.S.	

J.S.Moore
Major. A.D.V.S.
H.Q.V.S. 19th. Division.

Duplicate

WAR DIARY

~~INTELLIGENCE SUMMARY~~

Instructions regarding War Diaries and Intelligence Summaries are contained in F.S. Regs., Part II. and the Staff Manual respectively. Title pages will be prepared in manuscript.

.... of .... Major L. A. Moore ....

Sheet I.

Place	Date 1918 May	Hour	Summary of Events and Information	Remarks and references to Appendices
L.B. central (Sheet 2)	1		Inspected 364. Brigade Headquarters – 21.22. 9th L.Coy.R.E. – 574. Brigade H.B. –	
	2		Inspected 4th Shropshires and sent Journals authority hereby to 3rd M.T.S. – Inspected 5/S. Wales Borderers – 9th Cheshires. 8th Staffords. Conference of Veterinary Officers at Office.	
	3		Inspected 3rd Dec. 19th H.A.C. Divisional Machine Gun Bttn. 8 & L Gosters.	
	4		Called on A.H.Q.S. 22 Div. Corps and attended conference.	
	5		Routine work.	
	6		Inspected Signal Coy. – 4 Shropshires. – 57th & 50th Infantry Bdes. – 3 Dec. 19th H.A.C.	
	7		Inspected 22 Reinurals – owing to Shell fire 3rd M.V.S. moved to T.30.a.O.O.	
	8		Sheet 24. Matteined 2 captured German F.H. horses.	
	9		Routine work.	
	10		Inspected 5/S. Wales Borderers they having had 4 R. & 1 L.H. killed by Gas Shell. Ordered 4 others slightly gassed to 3rd M.V.S.	
	11		Routine work. Conference of Veterinary Officers at Office.	
	12		Called on A.H.Q.S. 2nd Corps. Inspected Signal Coy. – 4th Shropshires L.I. 9th H.Coy.R.E. – 3 Dec. H.A.C. – South West of Bordels.	
	13		Inspected 21.22. 9th L.Coy.R.E. – 574. & 580. Infty. Bdes. – Divnl. M. Gun Bttn.	
Bordecque.	14		Called on A.H.Q.S. 2nd Corps.	
	15		Moved to Bordecque.	
	16		Routine work – Inspected N.H.Q. & M.M. Remounts.	
	17		Inspected 51 Remounts.	
	18		Left Bordecque and entrained for new area.	
St Germain la Ville.	19		Travelling. Arrived at St Germain la Ville. Called on A.H.Q.S. 9th Corps.	

Duplicate.

Army Form C.2118.

WAR DIARY
or
INTELLIGENCE SUMMARY.

(Erase heading not required.)

of Major L.A. Moore, A.D.C. — 19th Division.   Sheet II

Instructions regarding War Diaries and Intelligence Summaries are contained in F.S. Regs., Part II. and the Staff Manual respectively. Title pages will be prepared in manuscript.

Place	Date 1918 May	Hour	Summary of Events and Information	Remarks and references to Appendices
St Germain la Ville	20		A.H.T.S. 94th Corps called Inspected Signals 84th H.A.R. animals with Lieut.	
	21		Inspected 81. 82. 94th & Cos. R.E. — 31st M.T.S. arrived at Depot.	
	22		Called on A.H.T.S. 94th Corps.	
	23		Horrengates from 2nd Corps called. Inspected the following units with Lieut. 81. 82. 94th & Cos. R.E. — Divisional Train — 88th Bde. R.H.A. — H.A.C. 94th Divnl. Signal Coy. 8 H.A.R. — Divisional Conference of Veterinary Officers at office.	
	24		Inspected Machine Gun Coys — 9th Cheshires — 56th Bde. H.Q. — 1/4th Kings Shropshire L.I. and 2nd E. Cos. R.E. (late 6th) Wilts.	
	25		Inspected 21 & 82 ng. & Cos. R.E. — Routine work	
	26		Inspected also Borderers — 81st Bde. H.Q. and ordered 2 horses suffering from tedidly & Surdness to 31st M.T.S.	
	27		Inspected 5/4th Infantry Bde. H.Q., 8 Brigade Transport.	
	28		Routine work.	
	29		Moved to Cuttery.	
	30		Moved to Jouvery.	
	31		Routine work.	

L. Moore
Major. A.D.C.
H.Q.H.T.S. 19th Division.

Major. A.D.C.
H.Q.H.T.S. 19th Division.

WAR DIARY

INTELLIGENCE SUMMARY

Army Form C. 2118.

WWMB 19 B M[?]
Major Gen. Moore A.D.S.

Place	Date 1918 May	Hour	Summary of Events and Information	Remarks and references to Appendices
L.13 Central (Sheet 27)	1.		Inspected 50th Brigade Headquarters – 81. 82. 94th L. Coy. R.E. – 89th Brigade H.Q. 10th Worcesters – Remainder of Lockers – 58th Brigade H.Q. – 9th Welsh – 9th West Sur. Rea. – 6th Liverp. & 19th Hussars at Machine Gun Cttee. Sheet L.	
	2.		Inspected 1/4th Shropshire L.I. and sent animals suffering from debility to 30th M.S.S. Inspected 51st Rifles Rangers – 9th Cheshires – 9th Welsh Fusiliers. Conference of Veterinary Officers at Office.	
	3.		Inspected 3 Dec 19th H.A.C. Nivaual Machine Gun Bttn. 8th Foresters. Called on A.H.S. 52nd Div. Corps and attended conference.	
	4.		Routine work.	
	5.		Routine work.	
	6.		Inspected Signal Coy. – 1/4th Shropshire L.I. – 5/4th & 152nd Infantry Bdes. – 3 Dec H.A.C. Inspected 22 Remounts – owing to deficien. 21st M.S.S. moved to F. 20. a. L.6. Sheet 27. Mastered & captured General WH. horses.	
	7.		Routine work.	
	8.		Inspected S.I.S. Wales Borderers. They have had 6 R. & L.H. animals killed by gas shells. Ordered 4 others slightly gassed to 31st M.S.S. Routine work. Conference of Veterinary Officers at Office.	
	9.		Called on A.H.S. 2nd Dec. Corps. Inspected Signal Coy. 1/4th Shropshire L.I. 94th L. Coy. R.E. 3 Dec. H.A.C. – 5th South Wales Borderers.	
	10.		Inspected 81. 82. 94th L. Coy. R.E. – 54th & 58th Infy. Bdes. Divy. Coy. Called on A.H.S. 2nd Ind. Corps.	
	11.		Moved to Bourbecque.	
	12.			
	13.			
Bourlecque	14.		Routine work. Inspected H.Q. & M.M.P. animals.	
	15.		Inspected 51 Remounts.	
	16.		Left Bourlecque and entrained for new area travelling.	
	17.		Arrived at St. Germain la Ville.	
St. Germain la Ville.	18.		Called on A.H.D.? 9th Corps.	
	19.			

Army Form C. 2118.

WAR DIARY
of
~~INTELLIGENCE SUMMARY~~

(Erase heading not required).

Instructions regarding War Diaries and Intelligence Summaries are contained in F.S. Regs, Part II. and the Staff Manual respectively. Title pages will be prepared in manuscript.

~~~~~~ Major J.a.s Moore. A.V.C.

Sheet I.

Place	Date 1918 May.	Hour	Summary of Events and Information	Remarks and references to Appendices
St Germain la Velle	20.		A.D.V.S. 8th Corps called. Inspected depots & H.W.R. animals with him.	
	21.		Inspected 81.82.94th & Cav. R.E. — 314th M.S. arrived at Crépy.	
	22.		Called on D.H.V.S. 8th Corps.	
	23.		Movements from 8th Corps called. Inspected the following Units with him 81.82.94th Cav. R.E. — Divisional Coy. & H.Q.C. — H.Q. Bde. R.A. — H.Q. 9th. Detail Signal Coy. & H.Q. R.R. animals. Conference of Veterinary Officers at Office.	
	24.		Inspected Machine Gun Bth, 19th Chevoder — 56th Bde. R.A. — 114th Field Coy. R.E. and 2nd Cav. (N) Wilts.	
	25.		Inspected 21st & 2nd Bug. & Corps R.E. — 17 Machine worth	
	26.		Shoud states Bordernes — 2/4th Bde. R.A. and ordered 2 horses suffering from Debility & Blindness to 314th M.B.C.	
	27.		Inspected 3/4th Enfantry Bde. H.Q. & Brigade Transport.	
	28.		Routine work.	
	29.		Moved to Cudemy.	
	30.		Moved to Hannery.	
	31.		Routine work.	

J.a.s M——
Major. A.V.C.
D.A.D.V.S. 19th Division.

WAR DIARY or INTELLIGENCE SUMMARY.

(Erase heading not required).

Army Form C. 2118.

Instructions regarding War Diaries and Intelligence Summaries are contained in F. S. Regs., Part II. and the Staff Manual respectively. Title pages will be prepared in manuscript.

10 Bun — Major E. ....

Place	Date	Hour	Summary of Events and Information	Remarks and references to Appendices
Cairo	June 13		Assumed duties of D.A.D.V.S. 10th Division.	
	14		Inspected 3rd M.V.S. on 10th Divisional on 14th R. Blue Jackets L.I., on 9th Leinsters on 5/3rd R.E. on 8th Roy R.E.	
	15		Inspected 9th R. Irish Fus R.E., on 9th Kings on 9th Royal Irish, horses in stables, L.R. on 2nd South R.E. and 3rd Fuels Ambulance.	
	16		Inspected Divisional train on 2nd field and Mont e Biel Battalion	
	17		Inspected 31st M.T.S. Routine work.	
	18		Inspected 5th & 59th Ambulances	
	19		Inspected Divisional Headquarters signals & M.M.P. animals.	
	20		Conference of Veterinary Officers at Office.	
Maadment	21		Moved to Maadment.	
	22		Inspected 58th Brigade H.Q. 8 D.N. Staffords.	
	23		Inspected 8th & 9th Batt R.L.R. and H.Q. and L.F. and 9th Troops	

Army Form C. 2118.

WAR DIARY
INTELLIGENCE SUMMARY.
(Erase heading not required.)

Place	Date	Hour	Summary of Events and Information	Remarks and references to Appendices
Middelwick	24		Inspected 3 Coy. A.V.C. — 10 K.R. tunnels in O.K. Trenches on 82 day L. Coy. C.E. — 54 Fd. Bac. S.A.D.	Sheet II.
	25		Inspected 51. D. S.B. — O.K. L Coy. C.E. — 546 L Ambulance on 9th Bearer in 142 Rings Shropshire L.I.	
	26		Inspected 2nd Welsh — 9th Royal West Surrey — F.D. 58 L. Fr. Bde — 59 L Ambulance — 9 K. Welsh — Car. O.R.B.	
	27		Inspected H.S.S. Signals and M.T.R. animals transport Veterinary Officers at office.	
	28		Inspected 9 K.L. Loy. C.E. and Machine Gun Battalion	
	29		Attending conference at II corps Headquarters. Inspected 3/4 M.F.S.	
	30		Routine work.	

J. McMillin.
Major. A.V.C.
H.Q.H.S.D., 9 H. Division.

WAR DIARY
INTELLIGENCE SUMMARY

Place	Date	Hour	Summary of Events and Information	Remarks and references to Appendices
Burio	13.		Assumed duties of D.D.V.S. of 19th Division	
	14.		Inspected 3/4 M.F.S. — 9th Cavalry — 14th Hrs — 10th Hussars — 10th Hussars R.E. — Supply Coy. 9th Cavalry — S.S. & B — 8/24.	
	15.		Inspected 97th L. Coy. S.E. — O.R. detail — 3 Section H.A.C. — Army L. Coy. S.E. & 59th Field Ambulance	
	16.		Inspected Divisional Train and 24th Divl. & Machine Gun Battalion.	
	17.		Inspected 3/4 M.F.S. Farriers work.	
	18.		Inspected 54th & 59th L. Ambulances.	
	19.		Inspected Divisional Headquarters, Signals & R.M.P. Annex.	
	20.		Conference of Veterinary Officers of Force.	
	21.		Moved to Maudement.	
Maudement	22.		Inspected 83rd Divnal. H.Q., 88th M. Chaffeurs	
	23.		Inspected 87th & 88th Batts. R.H. and L.A.C. and 2/4 T.M. 2/4 Brigade.	

Army Form C. 2118.

WAR DIARY
or
INTELLIGENCE SUMMARY.

(Erase heading not required.)

Instructions regarding War Diaries and Intelligence Summaries are contained in F. S. Regs., Part II. and the Staff Manual respectively. Title pages will be prepared in manuscript.

_____ of _____ Major. E. Vaughan _____

(Sheet 1)

Place	Date 1918 June	Hour	Summary of Events and Information	Remarks and references to Appendices
Mondicourt	24.		Inspected 3 Coy. A.S.C. — 10th F. Ambulance — 8th Stokes 22nd F. Amb. R.E. — 57th F. Amb. R.A.	
	25.		Inspected 3 F.A.S.B. — 2nd F. Coy R.E. — 57th F. Ambulance — 9th Creches — 14th Stokes (Shropshire L.I.)	
	26.		Inspected 2 no. Widths — 9th F. Ambulance — 9th Royal Irish Fusiliers on the 57th F. Amb. — 57th F. Ambulance — 9th R.A. Road & L.& M. Coy. A.S.C.	
	27.		Inspected D.V.B. Remounts — M. Animals Conference.	
	28.		Veterinary Officers at Office.	
			Inspected 94th F. Coy R.E. & Machine Gun Battalion	
	29.		Attended conference at X Corps Headquarters. Inspected 5/4 M.T.S.	
	30.		Routine work.	

E. Vaughan.
Major. A.S.C.
H.Q. A.T.S. 19th Division

Army Form C. 2118.

WAR DIARY
INTELLIGENCE SUMMARY
(Erase heading not required)

of Major. E. Franklin. A.D.V.S.
D.A.D.V.S., 9th Division.

Week I. 3/6

Instructions regarding War Diaries and Intelligence Summaries are contained in F.S. Regs., Part II. and the Staff Manual respectively. Title pages will be prepared in manuscript.

Place	Date 1918 July	Hour	Summary of Events and Information	Remarks and references to Appendices
Monchaux	1.		Entrained for new area.	
	2.		Arrived at Tauguenbergues.	
Tauguenbergues	3.		Inspected Divisional Headquarters Signal Coy. and M.M.P.	
	4.		" 3/4 M.V.S., 9th Welsh, 5th S. Wales Borderers, Nov. 16th & 157th Companies A.S.C. Conference of Veterinary Officers at Office.	
	5.		Routine work.	
	6.		Selected new site for 3/4 M.V.S., D.D.V.S. 5th Army called	
	7.		Inspected 2nd South Wales Borderers, 11th Kings Shropshire Light Infantry, 56th Supply Bde. H.Q., 155th Coy. A.S.C.— 57th F. Ambulance, 9th Cheshires and 9th R. Scots Fusiliers.	
	8.		Inspected Divisional Headquarters Signal Coy. 27th F. Ambulance, 156 Coy. A.S.C., 9th Gordons, 2nd Worcesters, 57th Bde. H.Q., 104th Taumieks and 82nd Sup. Coy. R.E.	
	9.		Inspected 3/4 M.V.S. with D.D.V.S. 5th Army.	
	10.		" D.D.V.S. 5th Army some units of the Portuguese Army.	
	11.		Headquarters R.A., 84th Bde. R.F.A. and 88th Bde. R.F.A.	
	12.		Conference of Veterinary Officers at Office.	
	13.		Moved to Bouny.	
Bouny	14.		Inspected Divl. Headquarters Signal Coy. & M.M.P.	
	15.		" 84th & 88th Bdes. R.F.A. " 88th F. Bde. R.F.A. with A.D.V.S., 63th Corps.	

Army Form C. 2118.

WAR DIARY
of
INTELLIGENCE SUMMARY
(Erase heading not required.)

of Major. E. Franklin. A.V.C.
D.A.D.V.S., 19th. Division.

Sheet II

Instructions regarding War Diaries and Intelligence Summaries are contained in F.S. Regs., Part II. and the Staff Manual respectively. Title pages will be prepared in manuscript.

Place	Date 1917 July	Hour	Summary of Events and Information	Remarks and references to Appendices
Bony.	16.		Inspected 9th F. Coy. R.E., 9th Royal Welsh Fus., 58th Bde. H.Q., 9th Welsh, 2nd Wilts, 157 Coy. A.S.C. and 59th L. Ambulance.	
	17.		D.A.D.V.S. 3rd. Army & A.D.V.S. 13th. Corps inspected 31st M.V. Section. Attended conference at Corps re. Shipping.	
	18.		Inspected D.A.C. with D.D.V.S. & A.D.V.S. Conference of Veterinary Officers at Office.	
	19.		Inspected Divl. Headquarters, Signal Coy, M.M.P. & 15th Coy. A.S.C.	
	20.		9th L. Ambulance — 2nd Wilts. — 9th R. Welsh Fus. — 59 F. L. Ambulance — D.A.C. with D.D.V.S. 5th. Army.	
	21.		Inspected 8th. N. Staffords, 4th. Kings Shropshire L.I. — 13th Coy A.S.C., 57th L. Ambulance — 56th Bde. H.Q.	
	22.		Attended at 31st. M.V.S. and acted as President on Board inspecting cold stores.	
	23.		Inspected 84th Bde. R.F.A. — 59th L. Ambulance, — 159 Coy. A.S.C. — 9th. Royal Welsh Fus. with A.D.V.S. 18th. Corps.	
	24.		Inspected Divisional Headquarters, Signal Coy, — Headquarters R.A., — M.M.P.	
	25.		Inspected 88th Bde. R.F.A. Conference of Veterinary Officers at Office.	
	26.		Inspected 87th & 88th Brigades R.F.A. with A.D.V.S. 5th Army.	
	27.		8th. & 82nd. Coys. A.S.C. — 5th. S. Wales Borderers, 8th. Leaders, 57th Bde. H.Q., 156 Coy. A.S.C., & 9th. Leaders with A.D.V.S. 13th Corps.	

D. D. & I. L., London, E.C.
(A8001) Wt. W1771/M2931. 750,000 5/17 Sch. 52 Forms/C2118/14

WAR DIARY

Army Form C. 2118.

of — Major. E. Franklin. A.D.S.
D.A.D.V.S., 19th Division.

Month July 1917

Place	Date	Hour	Summary of Events and Information	Remarks and references to Appendices
Bavinc.	28.		Inspected Divisional Headquarters, M.M.P., — Divisional Mounted Detachment and Signal Coy.	
	29.		Inspected Divisional Machine Gun Battalion and 3rd. Mobile Veterinary Section.	
	30.		Inspected 154 Coy. A.S.C. — 59th F. Ambulance — Divisional Headquarters, 58th F. Ambulance and Signal Coy. with D.D.V.S., 5th Army.	
	31.		Acted as judge at Divisional Horse Show.	

E. Franklin.
Major. A.D.S.
D.A.D.V.S., 19th Division.

Army Form C. 2118.

WAR DIARY
INTELLIGENCE SUMMARY

of Major. E. Franklin. A.V.C.
D.A.D.V.S., 19 Division.

Sheet I

Place	Date 1918 July	Hour	Summary of Events and Information	Remarks and references to Appendices
Movement.	1.		Entrained for new area.	
Tanqueburgues.	2.		Arrived at Tanqueburgues.	
	3.		Inspected Divisional Headquarters, Signal Coy. 8 M.M.P. 3/H. M.T.S., 9 H. Welsh F/C. Watch Pards, 15H & 157 Coy. A.S.C. Conference	
	4.		of Veterinary Officers at Office.	
	5.		Routine work.	
	6.		Selected new site for M.D.S., Q.D.V.S. called.	
	7.		Inspected 11H H. Cheshire D., 56H Bde. H.Q., 155 Bay. A.S.C. - 57 H. Ambulance -	
	8.		9H Cheshires, 8H H. Stafford.	
	9.		Inspected Q. H. S. Signal Coy. - 58 H Bde. A.S.C. - 15 b Bay A.S.C. - 8H.	
	10.		Cheshires - 3rd H. Worcesters - 157 Bde. H.Q., 10 H. P. Warwicks & 8 Way. of Coy. R.E.	
	11.		Inspected 2/4H. M.D.S. with D.D.V.S., 5H. Army.	
	12.		Some visits of Tanqueur Army with Q.Q.V.S.	
			Headquarters, R.A., 87H Bde. R.S.A., Conference of D.V.S.	
Bouy.	13.		Moved to Bouy.	
	14.		Inspected Divisl. Headquarters, Signal Coy. 8 M.M.P.	
	15.		9H. & 88H. Bdes. R.F.A.	
	16.		Divis. Med. Department. Inspected 88H. Bde. R.F.A. with A.D.V.S. 13H Carps.	
			9H. Field E., 9H. Royal Welsh Fus., 58H Bde. H.Q., 9H. Welsh, 2 May.	
	17.		D.A. Cay. A.S.C. and 59 H. L. Ambulance.	
	18.		With 157 Coy. A.D.V.S. inspected 81H. M.D.S. attended conference on Clipping.	
	19.		A.D.V.S. 13H Corps Headquarters.	
	20.		Inspected D.A.C. with D.D.V.S. & A.D.V.S. Conference of Veterinary Officer.	
			D.D.V.S., Signal Coy., M.M.P. and 13H. Coy. D.A.C.	
	21.		9H. Cheshires - 2nd. Wilts - 9H. R.W. Fusiliers - 59H. L. Ambulance - &	
			S.A.C. with D.D.V.S. 5H. Army.	
			Inspected 7H. H. Hants, 7H. H. Cheshire L.I. - 11H. H. Cheshire L.I. - 155 Bay. A.S.C. - 57H. H.	
			Ambulance and 56H. Bde. Headquarters.	

Army Form C. 2118.

WAR DIARY

of — Major E. Franklin. A.D.C.
D.A.D.V.S., 19th Division

Instructions regarding War Diaries and Intelligence Summaries are contained in F.S. Regs., Part II. and the Staff Manual respectively. Title pages will be prepared in manuscript.

Place	Date 1918 July	Hour	Summary of Events and Information	Remarks and references to Appendices
Bavai	22.		Attended at 3 P.M. M.S. and acted as President on board looking cold stores. Sheet II	
	23.		Inspected 87th Bde. R. Sta. — 59th F. Ambulance — 157 Coy. A.S.C. — 9th R.W. Fus with A.D.V.S.; 13th Corps.	
	24.		Inspected Q.M.S.; Signal Coy. — Headquarters R.A. — M.M.P. 88th Bde. R. Sta.; Conference of Veterinary Officers 87th Bde. & 88th Bde. R. Sta. with D.D.V.S., 5th Army	
	25.		" 9th Bde. & 82nd F. Coo. R.E., 5th F.D. Bearers — 8th F. Bearers — 57th Bde. M.B. 9th & 8 9th F. Batteries with A.D.V.S., 13th Corps.	
	26.		156 Coy. A.S.C. & 9th F. Bearers with A.D.V.S., 13th Corps.	
	27.		Inspected Divnl. Headquarters, M.M.P. — Mounted Detachment & Signal Coy. Machine Gun Bttn. and M.T.S.	
	28.		" 157 Coy. A.S.C. — 59th F. Ambulance — Q.M.S.; 8 Signal Coy with A.D.V.S., 13th Corps.	
	29.			
	30.			
	31.		Acted as judge at Divisional Horse Show.	

E. Franklin
Major. A.D.C.
D.A.D.V.S., 19th Division

Army Form C. 2118.

WAR DIARY
INTELLIGENCE SUMMARY.

of Major E. Lauritin. A.D.V.S.
D.A.D.V.S., 19th Division

Instructions regarding War Diaries and Intelligence Summaries are contained in F.S. Regs., Part II. and the Staff Manual respectively. Title pages will be prepared in manuscript.

Place	Date	Hour	Summary of Events and Information	Remarks and references to Appendices
Bavy	1		Inspected 82nd L. Coy. R.E. — 174th F.A. Drapostive L.S. — 9th N. Staffords — 57th F. Ambulance — 367th Suppy. Bde. — 155th Coy. A.S.C. — with D.D.V.S. 9th Division —	Sheet I
	2		Routine work	
	3		Staying at H.Q. 4th Divisional Horse Show.	
	4		D.D.V.S. 5th Army inspected 314th M.V.S.	
	5		Called on A.D.V.S. 3rd Division and arranged to take over site of 3rd Div. M.V.S.	
	6		Inspected Divisional Headquarters, M.M.P. and Mounted Detachment.	
	7		Moved to Laventerre.	
Laventerre	8		Inspected 8th Bde. R.T.A. Conference of Veterinary Officers at Office.	
	9		8th, 82nd, 94th Coy. R.E. — W Cable Section 9. E. — 88th Bde. R.T.A.	
	10		9th Welsh — Ind. Welsh — 9th Royal Welsh Fus. — 58th Suppy. Bde. M.G. — and 314th M.V.S.	
	11		Routine work. Inspected Divisional Headquarters & Signal Coy.	
	12		Inspected 9th Cheshires — 367th Suppy. Bde. M.G. — 88th N. Staffords — 174th R. Drapostive L.S.	
	13		4th Bde. R.F.A. — H.Q. & 2 Dec. 17th D.A.C.	
	14		9th Welsh — 14th Kings Drapostive L.S. — 88th N. Staffords — 314th M.V.S. with A.D.V.S. 13th Corps.	
	15		Inspected Machine Gun Btty. — Signal Coy. — Cable Section R.E. — Conference of Veterinary Officers at Office.	
	16		Inspected 65 remounts. Called by A.D.V.S. 13th Corps.	
	17		D.A.Q. — 5th South Wales Borderers.	
	18		5th L. Ambulance — 57th Suppy. Bde. M.G. — 3rd Worcesters — 10th R. Warwicks — and 9th Cheshires.	
	19		Routine work. Inspected 88th Bde. R.T.A.	
	20		Inspected Signal Coy. — 57th & 58th L. Ambulances. — 155 - 156 - 157 Coo. A.S.C. — 314th M.V.S. —	
	21		Inspected 8th 88th Bdes. R.T.A. — 176th Yeomanry Coy. R.E.	
	22		Divisional Headquarters — 81st Hay R.E. — Conference of Veterinary Officers	
	23		314th M.V.S. — 9th Coy. R.E. and Divisional Mounted Detachment.	

Army Form C. 2118.

WAR DIARY
INTELLIGENCE SUMMARY.
(Erase heading not required)

of Major E. Franklin. A.D.C.
D.A.D.V.S., 19th Division.

Instructions regarding War Diaries and Intelligence Summaries are contained in F.S. Regs., Part II. and the Staff Manual respectively. Title pages will be prepared in manuscript.

Place	Date	Hour	Summary of Events and Information	Remarks and references to Appendices
	1917 August		Sheet II	
Laberviere	24.		Inspected W Cable Section R.E. — Signal Coy. — 159th H. Btty. R.F.A. — 82nd L. Coy. R.E.	
	25.		3/4 M.T.S. — N. Gun Batty. — 798 Labour Coy.	
	26.		162 Labour Coy. — H.Q. 59th Labour Group — 59th L. Ambulance — 87th Bde. R.F.A.	
	27.		Inspected 31 M.T.S. — W Cable Section R.E. — Signal Coy. — 56th Supply Bde. H.Q. — 8th M. Stafford — 1/4th N. Shropshire L.I. — 9th Cheshires.	
	28.		Inspected 2nd Wilts — 9th Welsh Fus. — 57th Supply Bde. H.Q. and 57th Supply Bde. R.F.A. — 58th Supply Bde. H.Q. and 58th Supply Bde. 3rd Worcesters — 10th R. Warwicks. — 8th South Wales Borderers — 8th Leacher.	
	29.		Inspected Divl. Headquarters — Signal Coy. — M.M.P. Conference of Veterinary Officers at Office.	
	30.		Inspected 155 - 156 - 157 Coy. A.S.C. — No. 1 Coy. 14th Divl. Train.	
	31.		3 Sec. D.A.S. Mounted Detachment. Routine work.	

R. Franklin
Major. A.D.C.
D.A.D.V.S., 19th Division.

Army Form C. 2118.

WAR DIARY

INTELLIGENCE SUMMARY

of — Major. E. Franklin. A.V.C.
A.D.V.S. 19th Division

Instructions regarding War Diaries and Intelligence Summaries are contained in F.S. Regs, Part II. and the Staff Manual respectively. Title pages will be prepared in manuscript.

Place	Date 1918 August	Hour	Summary of Events and Information	Remarks and references to Appendices
Bouzy	1		Inspected 22nd Hvy. Bty. R.E. – 1/4th King Shropshire L.I. – 8th N. Staffords – Sheet I	
			57th L. Ambulance – 56th Suffy. Bde. H.Q. – 155 Bgy. A.D.D.L. with O.D. D.V.S. 5th Army.	
	2		Routine work	
	3		Staying at No 6 Divisional Horse Show	
	4		O.D.V.S. 5th Army inspected 3rd M.D.S.	
	5		Called on O.A.D.V.S. 3rd Division and arranged to take over side of 3rd Div. M.D.S.	
	6		Inspected Divisional Headquarters. M.M.P. and Mounted Detachment.	
	7		Moved to Labeuvriere	
Labeuvriere	8		Inspected 87th Bde. R.S.A. Conference of Veterinary Officers at Office.	
	9		" 81st, 82nd, 9th, L. Bgy. Bs. R.E. – Cable Section R.E. – 88th Bde. R.S.A.	
	10		" 9th Welsh – 2nd Wilts – 9th Royal Welch F.us. – 58th Suffy. Bde. H.Q. 8	
			3/4th M.D.S.	
	11		Routine work. Divisional Headquarters & Signal Coy. inspected	
	12		Inspected 9th L. Centures – 56th Suffy. Bde. H.Q. – 8th N. Staffords	
	13		" 4th Bde R.S.A. – 1/4th K. Shropshire L.I. D.A.C.	
			" 9th Welch – 1/4th Kings Shropshire L.I. – 8th N. Staffords – 3/4th M.D.S. with	
	14		A.D.V.S. 5th Army. 9/3rd. troops	
	15		Inspected Machine Gun Batt. – Signal Coy. – Cable Section R.E. Conference of	
			Veterinary Officers at Office.	
	16		Inspected Dismounted Section called on A.D. V.S. 13th Corps.	
	17		" D.A.C. – 5th South Wales Borderers	
	18		" 39th L. Ambulance – 57th Suffy. Bde. H.Q. – 3rd troops – 10th L. Daniels	
			and 8th Blokers.	
	19		Routine work. Inspected 88th Bde. R.S.A.	
	20		" 57th & 58th L. Ambulances — 155·156·157 Cos A.C.C. – 3/4th M.D.S. –	
			Inspected Signal Coy. – 176th Tunnelling Coy. R.E.	
	21		" Cable Section R.E.	
	22		" 87th & 88th Rdes. R.S.A. – 176th Tunnelling Coy. R.E.	
			" Divl. Headquarters – 81/4th L.Bgy. R.E. Conference of Veterinary Officers.	
	23		" 3/4th M.D.S. – 9th L. Bgy. R.E. & Divisional Mounted Detachment.	

D.D. & L., London, E.C. (A800.) Wt. W1771/M2031 750,000 5/17 Sch. B2 Forms/C2118/14

Army Form C. 2118.

WAR DIARY
INTELLIGENCE SUMMARY.
(Erase heading not required)

of Major E. Franklin. A.D.C.
D.A.D.V.S., 19th Division.

Instructions regarding War Diaries and Intelligence Summaries are contained in F.S. Regs., Part II. and the Staff Manual respectively. Title pages will be prepared in manuscript.

Place	Date 1918 August	Hour	Summary of Events and Information	Remarks and references to Appendices
Lateuviere	24		Inspected M Cattle Section R.E. — Signal Coy. — 159 H. Bty. R.G.A. — 82 Mdy. Lay. R.E. Sheet II.	
"	25		" 3/4 M.V.S. — M. Gun Battalion — 190 Labour Coy.	
"	26		" 87th Bde. R.G.A. — 162 Labour Coy. — H.8, 89 H. Labour Group. — 59 H.L. Ambulance —	
"	27		Inspected 31 M.V.S. — M Cattle Section R.E. — Signal Coy. — 56 H. Supply Coy. H.Q. 8 H. N. Stafford. L 114 H.L. Shropshire L.S. — 9 H. Cheshires.	
"	28		Inspected 2nd Wilts — 9 H. Devot. — 9 H. R.W. Fusiliers — 58 H. Supply Coy. H.S. 5 H. South Wales Borderers — 57 H. Supply Bde. H.S. — 8 H. Gloster — 3rd Worcesters — 10 H. R. Warwicks.	
"	29		Inspected Divnl. Headquarters — Signal Coy. & M.M.P. Conference of Veterinary Officers at Office.	
"	30		Inspected 155·156·157 Coy. A.S.C. — No.1 Coy. 14 H. D.S. Train.	
"	31		" 3 Sec. S.A.C. — Mounted Detachment. Routine work.	

J. Franklin
Major. A.D.C.
D.A.D.V.S., 19th Division.

ADVS 19 D Army Form C. 2118.
Major E. Frankling A.V.C.
Vol 38

WAR DIARY
INTELLIGENCE SUMMARY
(Erase heading not required)

Place	Date	Hour	Summary of Events and Information	Remarks and references to Appendices
Labeuvrière	1918 Sept. 1.		Inspected 38th Field Ambulance, 2 Sec. 19th D.A.C.	
"	2.		9th F. Coy R.E., 1 Sec. 19th D.A.C. selected new site for M.D.S.	
"	3.		47th Bde. R.F.A., 2 Sec. 19th D.A.C., 3 Sec. 22 Army Que. L.F. Coy.	
"	4.		with A.D.V.S. 13th Corps.	
"	5.		Inspected Divisional Headquarters, 726 Labour Coy, 817th Labour Coy.	
"	6.		Routine work. Conference of Veterinary Officers at Office.	
Béthune	7.		Moved to Grand Santé, Béthune.	
"	7.		Inspected Machine Gun Bttn, 58th Inf. Bde. H.Q., 2nd Wilts, 9th Welsh, 9th Royal Welsh Fusiliers, 57th Inf. Bde. H.Q., 10th R. Warwicks, 13 rd Worcesters, 8th Gloucesters.	
"	8.		Inspected Signal Coy, 56th Suff. Bde. H.Q., 9th Cheshires, 14 Ships Shropshire L.I., 8th N. Staffords.	
"	9.		Inspected 87th Bde. R.F.A. Attended at 51 M.D.S. when D.D.V.S. 5th Army inspected a number of animals for casting.	
"	10.		Inspected 57th & 59th Field Ambulances, 81st Coy. R.E. & 19th Signal Coy.	
"	11.		88th Bde. R.F.A. & 5th S.W. Borderers.	

Army Form C. 2118.

WAR DIARY
~~INTELLIGENCE SUMMARY~~
(Erase heading not required).

of Major. E. Franklin. P.V.O.

Instructions regarding War Diaries and Intelligence Summaries are contained in F. S. Regs., Part II. and the Staff Manual respectively. Title pages will be prepared in manuscript.

Place	Date	Hour	Summary of Events and Information	Remarks and references to Appendices
Bethune	1918 September 12.		Inspected A/H & B. Bde. R.F.A., C/H R. Bde. R.F.A. Conference of Veterinary Officers at Office.	
"	13.		Inspected 2 Div. 14 R. D.F.C. B & D. Btys H & R. Bde. R.F.A., A & D. Btys. H R. Bde. R.F.A. & 9 R. F. Coy. R.E.	
"	14.		Inspected H Q 2 F. Coy. R.E., 58 R. F. Ambulance & M.M.P.	
"	15.		9 R. Signal Coy, 2 Lee, 9 R. D.F.C. 82 F. Coy. R.E. & H S. D.F.C	
"	16.		H R. Bde. R.F.A. with A.D.V.S. 13 R. Corps.	
"	17.		Divisional Headquarters & Mounted detachment.	
"	18.		88 R. Bde. R.F.A. with A.D.V.S. 13 R. Corps. Routine work.	
"	19.		56 R. Inf. Bde. H.S., 1/4 R. H.S.L.L., 8 R. N. Staffords, 9 R. Cheshires	
"	20.		Conference of Veterinary Officers at Office.	
"			Inspected No. 1 Dec. 19 R. D.F.C. Examined 101 Remounts for the Division.	
"	21.		Inspected 58 R. Inf. Bde. H.S., 9 R. R. Welsh Fus., 2 ndy. Wilts., 9 R. Welsh 8 31/4 M.T.B.	
"	22.		Inspected 57 R. Inf. Bde. H.S., 3 rd. Sonerers, 10 R. R. Warwicks & 8 R. Workes.	

Army Form C. 2118.

WAR DIARY
of Major. E. Franklin. A.V.C.

INTELLIGENCE SUMMARY
(Erase heading not required)

Place	Date 1918	Hour	Summary of Events and Information	Remarks and references to Appendices
Bethune	September 23.		Machine Gun Bttn. & Divisional Headquarters inspected.	
"	24.		Inspected 59th F. Ambulance, Signal Coy., D divisional Train & 81st M.T.S.	
"	25.		Inspected 87th Bde. R.F.A.; 81st & 94th 7. Cos. R.E.	
"	26.		Routine work. Conference of Veterinary Officers at Office.	
"	27.		Gave Lecture on Foot & Mouth Disease. Inspected 5th S.W.B.	
"	28.		Inspected 57th & 58th Field Ambulances & Signal Coy.	
"	29.		31st M.V.S. & M.M.P. Routine work.	
"	30.		R. Cable Sec. R.E. & Divisional Headquarters.	

E. Franklin
Major. A.V.C.
D.A.D.V.S. 19th Division

Army Form C. 2118.

WAR DIARY

INTELLIGENCE SUMMARY.

of Major E. Franklin. R.A.C.

Instructions regarding War Diaries and Intelligence Summaries are contained in F. S. Regs., Part II. and the Staff Manual respectively. Title pages will be prepared in manuscript.

Place	Date	Hour	Summary of Events and Information	Remarks and references to Appendices
	1918			
Labourne	September 1.		Inspected 58th Field Ambulance, 2 Sec. 19th D.A.C., 8 31st. M.T.S.	
"	2.		" 9th. 7 Coy. R.E., 1 Sec. 19th. D.A.C. Selected new site for M.T.S.	
"	3.		" 47th Bde. R.F.A., 2 Sec. 14th D.A.C, 3 Sec. 22 Army Ava. Hy. Coy.	
"	4.		With A.D.V.S., 13th Corps.	
"	5.		Inspected Divisional Headquarters, 105th Labour Coy. & 17th Labour Coy.	
"	6.		Routine work. Conference of Veterinary Officers at office. Moved to Canal South, Bethune.	
Bethune	7.		Inspected Machine Gun Bttn, 58th Suffy. Bde. F.S., 2nd Wilts, 9th Welch 9th. Royal Welch Fusiliers, 57th Suffy Bde. F.S., 10th R. Warwicks, 3rd Worcesters, 8 8th Worcesters.	
"	8.		Inspected Signal Coy, 56th Suffy Bde. F.S. 9th Cheshires, 11th Kings. Proposine F.C. 8 8th N. Staffords.	
"	9.		Inspected 87th Bde R.F.A. Attended at 21 M.T.S. when D.D.V.S. "Army" inspected a number of animals for casting.	
"	10.		Inspected 57th & 59th Field Ambulances, 87th, 7 Coy R.E. & 19th Signal Coy.	
"	11.		" 88th Bde. R.F.A. & 5th South Wales Borderers.	

Army Form C. 2118.

WAR DIARY of 1 Major. E. Franklin. A.V.C.

INTELLIGENCE SUMMARY.
(Erase heading not required.)

Place	Date	Hour	Summary of Events and Information	Remarks and references to Appendices
Bethune	1918 September 12		Inspected A/H.Q. Bde. R.F.A. Conference of Veterinary Officers at Office.	
"	13		Inspected 2 Sec. 14th. D.A.C., B.S.D. B.Hys. H.Q. Bde. R.F.A., A-8. D. B.Hys. 47th. Bde. R.F.A., 89th. 7 Coy. R.E.	
"	14		Inspected #32.7 Coy. R.E. 58th. Field Ambulance & M.M.P.	
"	15		19th. Signal Coy, 2 Sec. 19th. D.P.C., 82nd. 7. Coy. R.E. 8 St. 8., D.A.C.	
"	16		47th. Bde. 18th. R.F.A. with A.D.V.S. 13th. Corps.	
"	17		Divisional Headquarters & Mounted Detachment.	
"	18		88th. Bde. R.F.A. with A.D.V.S. 13th. Corps. Routine work R.	
"	19		56th. Supply Bde. H.S., 4th. A.S.C., 8th. N. Staffords. Qr. Stables.	
"	20		Conference of Veterinary Officers at Office. Inspected No. 1 Sec.) A.O. Examined 121 Remounts for the Division	
"	21		Inspected 58th. Supply Bde. H.S., 9th. R. Welsh Fus., 2nd. Wilts, 8.9.L. Welsh & 31st. M.T.O.	
"	22		Inspected 57th. Supply Bde. H.S., D.of Cornwalls, 10th. Warwicks, 8 St. Staffs.	

Army Form C. 2118.

WAR DIARY

~~INTELLIGENCE SUMMARY~~

of Major E. Franklin. A.V.C.

Instructions regarding War Diaries and Intelligence Summaries are contained in F. S. Regs., Part II. and the Staff Manual respectively. Title pages will be prepared in manuscript.

Place	Date	Hour	Summary of Events and Information	Remarks and references to Appendices
Bethune	1918 Septmber. 23.		Machine Gun Bttn. 8 Divisional Headquarters inspected.	
"	24.		Inspected 59th. 7. Ambulance, Signal Coy, Divisional Train 8.31.19. M.I.S.	
"	25.		Inspecting 8½ F. Rde. R. 7.19, 8.19, 894th. 7. Coo. R.E.	
"	26.		Routine work. Conference of Veterinary Officers at Office.	
"	27.		Gave lecture on Foot & Mouth Disease. Inspected 5th. S.W.B.	
"	28.		Inspected 57th. 8.58th. Field Ambulances 8. Signal Coy.	
"	29.		31st. M.I.S. 8 M.M.P. R. Routine work.	
"	30.		R. Cattle &c. R.E. 8. 1 Divisional Headquarters.	

E. Franklin
Major. A.V.C.
D.D.V.S., 19th Division

D.D.V.S., 19th Division

Duplicate

Army Form C. 2118.

Instructions regarding War Diaries and Intelligence Summaries are contained in F. S. Regs., Part II. and the Staff Manual respectively. Title pages will be prepared in manuscript.

WAR DIARY
INTELLIGENCE SUMMARY.

Major E. Franklin. A.V.C.

(Erase heading not required)

Sheet I.

Place	Date	Hour	Summary of Events and Information	Remarks and references to Appendices
Bethune.	1918. October. 1.		Inspected Divisional Headquarters & M.M.P.	
	2.		" 88 Bde. R.F.A. Conference of Veterinary Officers at Office.	
Quedel.	3.		Moved to Quedel.	
Stenu.	4.		" " Stenu.	
	5.		Routine work.	
	6.		Inspected Signal Coy. M.M.P. - Divisional Headquarters and Mounted Detachment.	
	7.		Routine work.	
	8.		Moved to Graincourt.	
Graincourt.	9.		" " Noyelles.	
Noyelles.	10.		Inspected 31 M.T.C. - 58 F. Ambulance - 5 H. S. W. B. - Conference of Veterinary Officers at Office.	
	11.		Inspected 56 Bde. Headquarters - 4 Shropshires - 8 H. M. Staffords - 9 H. Cheshires - 58 Bde. Headquarters - 2 Wilts - 9 H. Welch - 9 H. R. W. Fus.	
	12.		Inspected 67 F. Ambulance - 81 F. Coy. R.E.	

A6045. Wt. W14422/M1160. 35,000. 12/16. D.D.&L. Forms/C./2118/14.

Duplicate.

Army Form C. 2118.

Instructions regarding War Diaries and Intelligence Summaries are contained in F. S. Regs., Part II. and the Staff Manual respectively. Title pages will be prepared in manuscript.

WAR DIARY of Major E. Frank Die. A.V.C.

INTELLIGENCE SUMMARY

(Erase heading not required.)

Sheet 2.

Place	Date	Hour	Summary of Events and Information	Remarks and references to Appendices
	1918. October.			
Mayelles.	13.		Moved to Cambrai.	
Cambrai.	14.		Inspected 57 Bde. Headquarters – 8 F. Glosters – 10 F. Warwicks – Bdy. Worcesters – S Sec. D.T.C.	
	15.		Inspected Machine Gun Bttn. – Signal Coy. – Divisional H.Q.	
	16.		Conference with D.D.O.V.S., 2nd F. Division.	
	17.		" of Veterinary Officers at Office.	
	18.			
Avesnes-lez-Aubert.	19.		Moved to Avesnes-lez-Aubert. Inspected 5 F.A.D. B. – M.M.P. – Signal Coy.	
	20.		Moved to St. Aubert.	
St. Aubert.	21.		Inspected 81 – 82 – 94 F. Cos. R. E.	
	22.		" Mounted Detachment – 31 M.D.S. – Divisional Headquarters	
	23.		Moved to Avesnes-lez-Aubert. Inspected 1 & 2 secs. D.T.C.	
Avesnes-lez-Aubert.	24.		Inspected 57 Bde. H.Q. – 8 Bn. Worcesters – 8/ Glosters – 10 F. Royal Warwicks.	
	25.		Conference of Veterinary Officers at Office.	
	26.		Inspected 57 F. Ambulance – 15th Coy. A.S.C.	

Army Form C. 2118.

WAR DIARY
INTELLIGENCE SUMMARY
of Major. E. Franklin. D.V.C.

Sheet 3

Place	Date	Hour	Summary of Events and Information	Remarks and references to Appendices
France. Oct. 17th about 27.	1918 Oct. 27.		Inspected 58 Bde. Headquarters – 2 Siege – 9th. Welch – 9th. R. Royal Welch & waitlers.	
	28.		Inspected 57 Bde. Headquarters – 3rd. Worcesters – 8th. Gloster – 10th. R. Warwicks – 21 M.D.S.	
	29.		Inspected Machine Gun Battalion and 5th. South Wales Borderers – " 56 Bde. Headquarters – 11th. Shropshires – 8th. N. Staffords – 9th. Cheshires – 57th. F. Ambulance.	
	30.			
	31.		Inspected Signal Coy – D ac D.P.C. – Conference of Veterinary Officers at Office.	

[signature]
Major. D.V.C.
D.P.D.V.S., 19th. Division.

Army Form C. 2118.

RADVS19D

WAR DIARY of Major E. Franklin. R.V.C.

INTELLIGENCE SUMMARY.
(Erase heading not required.)

Place	Date	Hour	Summary of Events and Information	Remarks and references to Appendices
	October 1918			Sheet I.
Bethune	1.		Inspected Divisional Headquarters 8 M.M.P.	
	2.		" 88th Bde. R.F.A. Conference of Veterinary Officers at Office.	
	3.		Moved to Quostel.	
Quostel	4.		" Stain.	
Stain	5.		Routine work.	
	6.		Inspected Signal Coy - M.M.P. - Divisional Headquarters and Mounted Detachment.	
	7.		Routine work.	
	8.		Moved to Graincourt.	
Graincourt	9.		" Moyelles.	
Moyelles	10.		Inspected 31 M.T.S. - 58 F. Ambulance - 5 H.Q. S.W.B. - Conference of Veterinary Officers at Office.	
	11.		Inspected 56 Bde. Headquarters - 1/4 Shropshires - 8 N. Staffords - 9 H. Cheshires. - 58 Bde. Headquarters - 2 Wilts - 9 H. Welsh - 9 H. R.W. Fus.	
	12.		Inspected 57 Field Ambulance 8 & 1 F. Coy. R.E.	

Army Form C. 2118.

WAR DIARY

~of~ Major. E. Frantz Lie. M.V.O.

Sheet 5.

Instructions regarding War Diaries and Intelligence Summaries are contained in F.S. Regs., Part II. and the Staff Manual respectively. Title pages will be prepared in manuscript.

Place	Date 1918	Hour	Summary of Events and Information	Remarks and references to Appendices
Mayelles.	October. 13.		Moved to Cambrai.	
Cambrai.	14.		Inspected 57 Bde. Headquarters – 8th Glosters – 10th R. Warwicks. Bty. Doucedeio – 3 sec. D.A.C.	
	15.		Inspected Machine Gun Bttn – Signal Coy – Divisional H.Q.	
	16.		Conference with D.D.D.V.S. 24th Division	
	17.		" " of Veterinary Officers at Office.	
	18.		Moved to Avesnes-leg-Aubert.	
Avesnes Leg-Aubert.	19.		Inspected 54. & W.B. – M.M.P. – Signal Coy.	
	20.		Moved to St. Aubert. Inspected 17 S.B. Bttys. 88 Bde. R.F.A.	
St. Aubert.	21.		Inspected 21st, 82nd, 8, 94th. 2 Coys. R.E.	
	22.		" Mounted Detachment – 21 M.S.I. – Divisional H.Q.	
	23.		Moved to Avesnes- leg- Aubert. Inspected 1 & 2 secs. D.A.C.	
Avesnes-Leg-Aubert.	24.		Inspected 57 Bde. H.Q. – 8th Doucedeio – 8th Glosters – 10th R. Warwicks.	
	25.		Conference of Veterinary Officers at Office.	
	26.		Inspected 5/7.F.Ambulance – 15th Coy. D.S.C.	
			1/5/5 – /5/6 & /5/7 Cos. D.S.C.	

Army Form C. 2118.

WAR DIARY
— of —
~~INTELLIGENCE SUMMARY~~ Major. E. Franklin. A.V.C.
(Erase heading not required.)

Sheet 3

Instructions regarding War Diaries and Intelligence Summaries are contained in F. S. Regs., Part II, and the Staff Manual respectively. Title pages will be prepared in manuscript.

Place	Date 1918	Hour	Summary of Events and Information	Remarks and references to Appendices
Avesnes-les-Aubert	October 27.		Inspected 58 Bde. Headquarters – 2nd. Wilts – 9th. Welsh – 9th. Royal Welsh Fusiliers.	
	28.		Inspected 57 Bde. Headquarters – 3rd. Worcesters – 8th. Gloucesters – 10th. R. Warwicks – 31. M.T.D.	
	29.		Inspected Machine Gun Bttn & 5th. South Wales Borderers.	
	30.		5 Bde. Headquarters – 1/4 Shropshires – 8th. N. Staffords – 9th. Cheshires – 5/4th. F. Ambulance.	
	31.		Inspected Signal Coy. – 3 Sec. O.A.C. – Conference of Veterinary Officers at Office.	

E. Franklin.
Major. A.V.C.
D.A.D.V.S., 19th Division.

Army Form C. 2118.

WAR DIARY of Major. E. Frankling. R.V.C.

INTELLIGENCE SUMMARY

Sheet I.

Instructions regarding War Diaries and Intelligence Summaries are contained in F. S. Regs., Part II. and the Staff Manual respectively. Title pages will be prepared in manuscript.

Place	Date 1918	Hour	Summary of Events and Information	Remarks and references to Appendices
Avesnes. Seg. Huybert.	November 1.		Inspected 31 M.V.S. – M.M.P. – Divisional Mounted Detachment.	
	2.		Selected new site for 31 M.V.S.	
	3.		Moved to Sendegies.	
Sendegies.	4.		" " "	
Sepmeries.	5.		" " "	
Jenlain.	6.		" " "	
	7.		Inspected Divisional Headquarters – M.M.P. – Signal Coy.	
	8.		" 31 M.V.S. Conference of Veterinary Officers.	
			Moved to La Flamengrie.	
La Flamengrie.	9.		Inspected 58 & 7 Ambulances – 154 & 156 Coo. R.S.C.	
	10.		Moved to 45 supplies – le Petit.	
Saryues- le Petit.	11.		Inspected Headquarters 8 Ligne Coy.	
	12.		Routine work.	
	13.		Inspected 56 Bde. Headquarters – "H" Supplies – 8 F.N. Stafford–	
			9th. Cheshires – Conference of Veterinary Officers.	
	14.		Moved to Sendegies.	
Sendegies.	15.		" " Pieres.	

Army Form C. 2118.

WAR DIARY
— of —
INTELLIGENCE SUMMARY Major E. Frank Lis. R.A.V.C.

(Erase heading not required)

Sheet 2

Instructions regarding War Diaries and Intelligence Summaries are contained in F.S. Regs., Part II. and the Staff Manual respectively. Title pages will be prepared in manuscript.

Place	Date 1918	Hour	Summary of Events and Information	Remarks and references to Appendices
Pierre	November 16.		Routine work.	
	17.		Inspected Signal Coy. — M.M.P. — Divisional Headquarters — Mounted Detachment — 21 M.J.S.	
	18.		Inspected 89 Bde. Headquarters — 2nd Wilts — 9th Welsh — 9th Royal Welsh Fusiliers — 59 F. Ambulance.	
	19.		Inspected 155 Coy. R.A.S.C. — 58 F. Ambulance.	
	20.		" 3 Sec. D.A.P.C. — 157 Coy. R.A.S.C. — Machine Gun Bttn.	
	21.		" 10th R. Warwicks — 5th South Wales Borderers — 58th F. Ambulance — 81 F. Coy. R.E.	
	22.		Inspected 57 Bde. Headquarters — 8th Gloucesters — 3rd W. Borderers — 9th F. Coy. R.E.	
	23.		Inspected Divisional Headquarters — M.M.P. — 82nd F. Coy. R.E. Signal Coy. — 57th F. Ambulance.	
	24.			
	25.		Moved to Cambrai.	
Cambrai	26.		Inspected Detachment 5th Cav. Res. Regt. — Routine work.	
	27.		" Headquarters Conference of Veterinary Officers.	

A6945 Wt. W14422/M1160 35,000 12/16 D. D. & L. Forms/C./2118/14

Army Form C. 2118.

WAR DIARY of Major E. Fraustein. A.D.C.

INTELLIGENCE SUMMARY

Sheet 3

Place	Date	Hour	Summary of Events and Information	Remarks and references to Appendices
Maubeuge.	November. 1918. 28.		Moved to Maours.	
Maours.	29.		Inspected Signal Coy - Routine work.	
	30.		3. M.S.S. - Machine Gun Battalion	

B. Fraustein
Major. A.I.C.
O.C. D.I.S. 19th Division.

Duplicate.

Army Form C. 2118.

Instructions regarding War Diaries and Intelligence Summaries are contained in F.S. Regs., Part II. and the Staff Manual respectively. Title pages will be prepared in manuscript.

WAR DIARY ~~or~~ ~~INTELLIGENCE SUMMARY~~
(Erase heading not required).

of Major E. Franklin. A.V.C.

Sheet I.

Place	Date	Hour	Summary of Events and Information	Remarks and references to Appendices
Avesnes - les - Aubert	1918. Nover. 1.		Inspected 51 M.D.S. - M.M.P. - Divisional Mounted Detachment.	
	2.		Relieved and sick for 51 M.D.S.	
	3.		Moved to Sendegies.	
Sendegies.	4.		" " Sepmeries.	
Sepmeries.	5.		" " Jolain.	
Jolain.	6.		Inspected Divisional Headquarters - M.M.P. - Signal Coy.	
	7.		" 51 M.D.S. - Conference of Veterinary Officers.	
	8.		Moved to La Flamengrie.	
La Flamengrie	9.		Inspected 58 F. Ambulance - 154 & 156 Coys. R.S.C.	
	10.		Moved to Wargnies - le - Petit.	
Wargnies. Le - Petit.	11.		Inspected Headquarters - Signal Coy.	
	12.		Routine work.	
	13.		Inspected 56 Bde. Headquarters - 4th Cheshires - 8th N. Staffords. 9th Cheshires - Conference of Veterinary Officers.	
	14.		Moved to Sendegies.	
Sendegies.	15.		" " Reims.	

A6945 Wt. W14422/M1160 35,000 12/16 D.D. & L. Forms/C./2118/14.

Army Form C. 2118.

WAR DIARY
INTELLIGENCE SUMMARY.
(Erase heading not required.)

of — Major. E. Frank line. R.V.C.

Sheet 2

Instructions regarding War Diaries and Intelligence Summaries are contained in F.S. Regs., Part II. and the Staff Manual respectively. Title pages will be prepared in manuscript.

Place	Date	Hour	Summary of Events and Information	Remarks and references to Appendices
Rieux.	1918. November. 16.		Routine work.	
	17.		Inspected Signal Coy — M.M.P. — Divisional Headquarters — Mounted Detachment — 3¹ M.D.S.	
	18.		Inspected 38 Bde. Headquarters — 2nd Wilts. — 9th Welsh — 9th Royal Welsh Fusiliers — 39 F. Ambulance.	
	19.		Inspected 155 Coy. A.S.C. — 58th F. Ambulance.	
	20.		" 3 Sec. D.A.C. — 154 Coy. A.S.C. — Machine Gun Btty.	
	21.		" 10th R. Warwicks — 5th South Wales Borderers — 38th F. Ambulance — 81st F. Coy. R.E.	
	22.		Inspected 5⁴ Bde. Headquarters — 9th R. Worcesters — 3rd Worcesters — 9th F. Coy. R.E.	
	23.		Inspected Divisional Headquarters — M.M.P. — 82nd F. Coy. R.E. — Signal Coy — 57th F. Ambulance.	
	24.		"	
	25.		Moved to Cambrai.	
Cambrai.	26.		Inspected Detachment 5th Cas. Rec. Park. — Routine work.	
	27.		Headquarters. Conference of Veterinary Officers.	

Duplicate

Army Form C. 2118.

WAR DIARY ~~INTELLIGENCE SUMMARY~~

of — Major. E. Franklin. D.V.C.

Sheet 3

Instructions regarding War Diaries and Intelligence Summaries are contained in F. S. Regs., Part II. and the Staff Manual respectively. Title pages will be prepared in manuscript.

Place	Date	Hour	Summary of Events and Information	Remarks and references to Appendices
Cambrai.	November 28. 1918		Moved to Maours.	
Maours.	29.		Inspected Signal Coy. - Routine work.	
	30.		" 2 M.S.S. - Machine Gun Battalion.	

E. Franklin
Major. D.V.C.
D.D.D.V.S, 19th Division

www.ingramcontent.com/pod-product-compliance
Lightning Source LLC
Chambersburg PA
CBHW081402160426
43193CB00013B/2087